HOLOGRAPHIC WORLDS

I

GALACTIC VOICES AND THE COLLAPSE OF VERTICAL SOCIETY

Darrell D. Davisson, Ph.D.

Cover Image: ***NGC 2818***
Hubble Space Telescope,
Public Domain

'I DON'T WANT TO CHANGE YOUR MIND, I WANT TO CHANGE YOUR LIFE'

TABLE OF LOGS

Introduction

"If all the insects on the planet were destroyed,
    The earth would die.
"If all the animals on the planet were destroyed,
    The earth would die.
"If all the plants on the planet were destroyed,
    The earth would die.
"If all the humans on the planet were destroyed,
    The earth would thrive.

Navajo (Dineh) saying

Life on Spaceship Earth

A question on any adult's mind sooner or later is can I survive? If I can survive, can I thrive? And by the way, who is ME and who is THEE? Robert Buckminster Fuller called our planet "spaceship earth." Karl Sagan observed it as "a pale blue dot." A lot of people call it Hell and a lot of people live in a hell of one kind or another at the present time on this 'pale blue dot,' 'spaceship earth.' Some people have everything the people living in hell do not, but they still feel like they are living in a hell of one kind or another and by all definitions are.

Religion and wealth offer no more opiate solutions. Military and militant solutions incur greater damage than they cure. Least of all can any major social institutions of the modern world put their humpty dumpty back together again, ones they often broke "with extreme prejudice." "Bliss" is now officially found in junk food and soda pop. "Ecstasy" is a drug and *"If you have an erection lasting more than for hours, call your doctor."*

If Aliens Aren't So Bad...

Some say that our only real hope of salvation in the absence of religion, failed states, failed economies, and other drugs or delusions, is to look to some well-intentioned, compassionate extraterrestrials to lift us from our imminent demise.

After all, if they can fly as they have been recorded as having done, arriving from solar systems measurable in light years away; if these same alien visitors can make gigantic crop circles with crisp edges with bent, twisted, and unbroken barley and wheat stems, if they can send digitized messages and portraits in fields next to England's largest telescope, they must have solved problems like radiation poisoning, cancers of all kinds, wholesome nourishment without killing animals, a spectre of happiness that diminishes if not eliminates political wrangling, greed, mental and social illnesses, then we hope they are here to help.

Yes, it could be quite a good thing for most of us if such a dream were true. Others of us who siphon the earth for gas, oil, coal, water, chemicals, quick profit will most likely find that their greed and ecological violence to the planet will become rather unprofitable in the face of energy being drawn from the void of space. Here lies the greatest dilemma. Fuels drive global society. Without them, another economy has to arrive, and along with that absence of energy needs go the need to fight wars to protect and steal those resources from weaker countries and disenfranchised citizens who would prefer to preserve the planet from the global piracy of carbon fuels in the name of big profits, national productivity, and 'the global economy.'

Unlimited Energy

We must assume that aliens, extraterrestrials, already have solved the energy limitations of space-time travel in order to get here. Observers of the extraterrestrial phenomenon claim that in a single cubic centimeter of space resides enough energy to meet all of the earth's energy needs for a single day.

What a mess such a change in energy production would make of the tyranny of the energy moguls and

Wall Street speculation gamblers who, with near the speed of light, play money games with public and corporate money and deny any consequential effects of their profit-based speculations on the global ecosystem.

In addition to extraordinary access to unlimited energy, extraterrestrials might even have different theologies than those on earth or possibly none at all. We might not need armies to fight wars for material resources or ideological absolutes. And in a world without religion, we would be limited to fighting racial wars, unless we come to a timely conclusion that all life is sacred, that it is just as real in the smallest point of existence as it is in the greatest dimensions. With such a galactic, or healthy universal vision we might find it difficult to handle such outrageous possibilities with only our five senses and a partially evolved brain, youngsters that we are among the stars and galaxies of our universe.

Newcomers on the Astral Block

Our universe is claimed to be 13 plus billion earth years old, but our sun only six billion and the spaceship earth only four or four and a half. We are new on the astral block. Just imagine meeting someone whose culture has lasted for a billion years, a million, or even a few hundred thousand longer. Human "civilization," as we call it, is only measurable for about eight to nine thousand years.

What is this 'civilization' anyway, since we are all so miserable and doing things that we know are not only destructive but often suicidal individually and globally? Apart from natural instabilities, nothing is more unstable or a threat to itself than human beings to themselves. Leonardo da Vinci once wrote that he hoped there would someday be a better human being.

Based on the superficialities of news media each evening, one would have to conclude the human specie is deeply in trouble, in need of a savior in every profession on earth as one sun/agricultural-based resurrection god has become hardly enough.

Be Humble in the Face of Astral History

So, what would we do if we met a living organism with an intelligence and history not even measurable or comparable to ourselves--we lizard-brained humans with our small frontal lobes and our small *corpus colossum* where we do most of our processing? Being humble, I think, would be the first order of business. Listen a lot to what you might be told or transmitted by any alien being who does not threaten to eat or kill you.

We already know the military lizard-based mindset will try to kill anything it doesn't understand and that "intelligence agencies" or "inquisitions," and "secret courts" will attempt to imprison and suppress all knowledge of such an encounter, if there is one that can be admitted unless, of course, it can be first encapsulated and blessed by religious psychophants.

Fortunately for all humanity, we must realize that a being which can appear here across such mega-distances probably has the capacity of nullify the knee-jerk reactions of people who use surrogate penises in the form of guns, bullets, high energy ray guns, lasers, and rockets.

If all of the thousands of encounters with extraterrestrials that have been recorded and claimed appearing in a vast variety of situations and settings are, in fact, a "knock, knock, knocking on heaven's door," then we should perhaps oil the hinges with whatever capacity of thought we can muster. Then, opening the door slowly--though we may be scared frozen stiff--be humble, simple and peaceful.

Such a directive for newbies like us, standing on the beach of history as the Aztecs once did to welcome the ships of Cortez and his lustful, gold-hungry passengers, we might discover that others in the galaxy or universe have not only survived their own histories of greed, conquest, and near-annihilation, but have succeeded in developing their capacity for empathy and compassion with a knowledge base that would humble the greatest terrestrial minds.

For most well-advanced extraterrestrial visitors to our "pale blue dot," their major behavior toward us may be utter disinterest as suggested by Arthur C. Clark's several classics, or passing amusement, rather than conquest and subjugation that has been the pattern of the human specie as it has spread its presence over the planet.

Muse or Mentor, Messenger X

Messenger X (pronounced 'ex') is a mythical mentor, my muse, if you will. His or its name came to me out of the blue, perhaps from the X-Files. I don't know if I invented him or if he just chose me to be an ambassador or diplomat, to both welcome his and perhaps millions of other extra-terrestrial (perhaps even extra-galactic) visitors and to let my fellow earth people know that we are part of a very dynamic and vast universe in time and space.

A Slow Realization is Just a Defense

Once we realize we can travel greater than the speed of light, that one can have an I.Q. beyond anything we can measure for ourselves at this time, that life-spans can be measured in hundreds of years, that there are many ways of knowing and doing, that a joyful and fulfilling life can be lived without money or pecuniary profit as a measure of one's worth, we might then enter into a new level of existence and break down our delusional defenses of what we fear, thinking as we do, of domination and control.

Many humans have thought such an existence is possible, either on earth or in a heavenly afterlife, but have no idea of how to experience it, although thousands of ideas, illusions, and delusions have been tried. As hard as we try, mixing up lizard-brain control mechanisms with uncontrollable meetings of psychological and biological needs we need to describe what a better world or 'heaven' might be. That various fantasies of heaven is nevertheless a global phenomenon in the face of the limitations of a human life span.

Meeting with X

With that said, let me introduce you to my earlier conversations with X. The reader must know that there may or may not be a X. He, she, it is either a figment of my imagination or a voice that speaks through my keyboard, independently of me, or it is just me. Any of my former students in the history of art and architecture will recognize my description of three formal shapes of human survival geometries.

Perhaps there is an intervention going on to some degree between the actual writer and the content being presented. Those are issues for the reader to decide. What I do not want to do is to suggest that these words and ideas are exclusively of extraterrestrial origin, or worse, that I am pretending to be an extraterrestrial or channeling, which are in a number of venues found over the Internet. One measure of the pretentiousness of pseudo- other-worldly messengers can be found in the theatrics of names given and claims made, especially by formal religions.

If I were to meet (or have a semi-consciously meeting) with a mind that has thousands or tens of thousands of years of evolution behind it, then one might expect the bearer of information to be more sober and have a long-range perspective on the human condition based on knowledge of our history that is mega-historical in its appearance and structure.

Keeping Us from Destroying Ourselves and the Planet

By the same logic, no superior extraterrestrial intelligence is needed to inform us of extraterrestrial threats of potential self-destruction, as that prospect lies well on the conscience of any informed person. We already know the imminent destruction of earth by any spectrum of human forces from perpetual war, nuclear weapons, nuclear power generation, insecticides, global warming, fossil fuel dependencies, and psychological needs for control, profit, reinforcements of ego-centricities, and the like.

If you are looking for a promise of utopia to be brought about as an ultimate promise by the "Great Religions;" if you want to know what alien history or culture or cities look like, or answers to those global preoccupations with magical thoughts, Magical Thinking, and magical systems, then you may as well put down the book immediately. I will reserve that right for shamans, priests, and sycophants ubiquitous everywhere on this terrestrial orb.

Homo sapiens: 'Man Who Knows,' a Pretense

It is given that there is a fathomless depth of ignorance about what is and has been known and constantly evolving among we *homo sapiens* (man who knows). Those who cannot think at all and those that have been constrained to think in obedient, conventional religious/ideological/cultural or political ways, will suffer the greatest dissolution of their identity and self (psyche) by any encounter with any intelligence greater than their own.

So, meet my ally and mentor X. His presence came to me as I lay asking myself, why don't the ET's reveal themselves? We have right and a need to know. It is entirely their choice and their timing, although MJ-12 has succeeded in muddying that reality. However, for those of us who follow "conspiracies," and "science fiction," the evidence of alien presence is increasingly and unmistakably apparent in spite of denials on all fronts. Could it be that powers that be are aware such a premature introduction would change human history forever and cause more social, economic, and psychological chaos than the warped and damaged human mind itself, which already threatens humanity.

Taking Out the Trash

So, my questions to X are focused on what is or are Galactic Entities (GE's) plans with or for us. What is their hesitation at waiting to show themselves directly?

What is their intent? Or is everything that has happened in the last 68,000 to 100,000 years of human or semi-semi-human existence part of a highly planned, strategic, extraterrestrial guardianship, much like the "God the Father," "Allah," "Jehovah" or other attributed string-pulling, puppeteer deities. What some of us would consider a humanely conceived process at integrating humanity into the larger galactic and possibly inter-galactic universe would be something less humanized into perceptions of God(s) and heaven(s) to which humanity has been chained for thousands of years by gravity and grave ignorance?

We hang on to systems that fail, because we fail to imagine something more workable and fear of any variable of change. Our social systems never worked well in the whole of human history, but by accident or by supernatural intention, got us this far.

This dialogue is as much about that concept, introduced many years ago by Professor George Kubler but a good idea a little slow to become popularized. It is distinctly in contrast to Leslie White who chose to see the entire development of civilization based on technological innovation.

Between the revelations by the Hadron accelerator and quantum physics of smaller and smaller entities and forces in and composition of our physical universe, it is apparent there is a force permeating all levels of reality that's at once both unpredictable and unifying.

To some extent modern physics has inquired and answered something we have been told for millennia by many people who we considered to be enlightened; namely, that we are not alone, that there is something vastly better in the universe and our future is most likely transcendent, peaceful, eternal, as the 'Great Religions' have claimed. We may be tied to something incompre-hensibly beautiful, joyful, and extraordinarily powerful all-embracing, permeating the smallest entity from its magnificent revelations visible in the nighttime sky, the theories of black holes and supernovae and their exist-ence throughout the universe. That is my hope for us. Reading this "brave new world" fully integrated (holistic) where all benefit from the uses and discoveries of science and technologies might be the most important book any one can read standing as we are always on the beach of the future and future space.

November 2016
Tehachapi, California

LOG I

CONTACT: EPIPHANY

It seems like nearly every morning soon after waking up I think of some truth about the turmoil in the world and decide I will remember those little gems and write them down. For some reason, I always fall back to sleep and have vivid dreams, dreams I can never remember but their contents seem so important during the dream and upon awakening, most is forgotten.

One evening when I couldn't sleep, I decided to write down my latest late night/early morning illumination, my latest 'epiphany' as they say but when I started writing, I couldn't stop. At some time around four in the morning, I was getting sleepy, went back to bed, and had my usual REM time. When I awoke the next morning and looked at what I had written, I was astonished. I was writing in someone else's voice as well as my own. It was a *manifestation* (the actual meaning of *epiphany*) and here's what I found on my screen.

"I am X. My name, the name X, is not a metaphor, nor am I a god. Like you, I am a cosmic being and really have no name, at least it is not important, least of all for you to know...and already you cannot understand me. I will explain to you why I take no name later. For now, let us say that upon encountering something new and alien your first unconscious response is to freeze and go numb. Then, when consciousness returns, you abstract the event or phenomenon into a single word or short phrase. It's the way you humans control your world of thoughts and experiences, which seem incoherent unless you can create symbols, narratives, and words around them.

"Words give humans certainty and derive instantaneously from significant attributes drawn from a wide variety of sources to amend themselves to any otherwise unfathomable event. Most thoughts occur after an encounter with a

1

new idea. Stamp it, seal it with an image, a logo, or a word and you capture the event to be stored in collective memory. Remember, in your axiomatic Biblical source, "In the beginning was the Word."

"Are you with me, TED? My job is to entreat your mind-brain to grow a whole new set of synapses absent from both your pre-frontal cortex and the *corpus collossum* separating the right and left hemispheres. Although you still have a serpent brain, as likewise we have, yours is encoded to accept and develop this and other new brain compartments and addition, which make you somewhat maleable.

"We have developed these capacities naturally for ourselves over time Because of the special geometry of our planet and double sun orbits that have affected all of our physiognomic differences, you humans might assume a little anxiety in visual encounters.

"We prefer to use a term taken from your ancient Greek mythology, '*the Medusa effect*': You frieze like stone in terror at anything so new and shocking you cannot put the experience into a word or phrase. Our proportions are similar to yours, but, we do not have the same proportions almost universally found in humans known to you as *psi* .618 and *Psi* 1.618, ratios discovered by the ancient Egyptians but claimed by the ancient Greeks as applied to the proportions of their sculptures of the human figure. We do not communicate in oral tones for the most part, least of all in radio or microwaves, which Terran governments have spent billions trying to find us in deep space, when we were already right here!"

At this point in X's dialogue, I cautiously interrupted to interject some form of participation spontaneously saying outloud, rather than writing it on my keyboard:

> So how do you communicate with each other
> and you with us?

"Just like I am doing now with you. We converse telepathically. It is the most effective method as I receive your messy emotional language, of which you are not always aware, as well as your words. We have also connected with you earthlings in space-time since 1945 and since that time in the form of what you might call "grass art," or "crop circles." At least four different Extraterrestrial Biological Entities (EBE's as your military labels us) groups have used the crop circles to at least say '*hello*.'

"We also have no reason now to anchor the harmonic proportions of our bodies as humans do, either as a value of pure beauty (Polykleitos and Pythagoras, 5th C. BCE), or as a 'proof that God designed you' either in 'his own image' or that you were by a mirror of a 'god-like' nature (Michelangelo, 15th c. CE) or even that you have designed God in your own image. Every conclusion you have reached, as I have partially described, it is a partial truth wherein we are all prisoners until a greater truth is unveiled.

"Your genetics tell you that you must know more, given your brain size. Your beautiful but primitive minds tell you there are many more truly awesome things yet to be found. Unfortunately, you nurture and even enjoy the prison of your financial, social, and religious systems out of nothing more than fear and anxiety snaking up through your three brains.

"In these few moments I have provided basic warnings not to mythologize me, or anything else that you come to know unexpectedly or by subsequently knowing or becoming conscious that something has occurred or an image has appeared for which you have no immediate explanations.

"Before you ask, TED, we know these things about your mind-brain because of our vast accumulation of information on human anatomy, neurology, psychology, and terrestrial history, all of which necessitates the presence of EBE's, or more simply and more appropriately as GE's, Galactic Entities.

"For your peace of mind, our race has never abducted humans for purely anatomical dissections as some would have you believe, although it is possible other EBE's at some time or are doing so. More importantly, you pose a much greater threat to yourselves and to the harmony of inter-related galactic fields of energy and time-space than any external threat."

"We all participate in universal space-time conscious-ness in contrast to your parsed and fractured ideologies and self-destructive social standards based on your need for se-curity in your fear of pain, suffering, and extinction.

"All the while, your physicists experiment with the ti-niest particles of matter/energy in hopes of finding the rea-son for being, your search for "God" and a rational explana-tion of why you are here. Such experiments even put your planet and the galaxy as a whole in jeopardy while you search in vain for a greater truth. Your militaries threatened all life on your planet with nuclear and biological weapons, by each and all nuclear power plants, deluding yourselves with prosaic phrases like '*atoms for peace.*'

"Your economic system costs millions of lives annually and at every step annihilates the possibility of a free creative growth even though you have the 'civilizing' pretext of sup-porting 'the arts.' Your country in particular objects to vio-lence, but is the most violent country on earth. Your govern-ment decries human brutality, but will not sign any agree-ments to ban land mines, cluster bombs, or closing foreign torture chambers.

"Twenty-seven million of your fellow Terrans (earth-lings) live in abject slavery. Millions of others live in finan-cial servitude and multiple cultures and religions identify women as inferior human beings, enslaving women to their husbands, and demean them sexually. In a number of Near Eastern and African religions and cultures, men are edu-cated to believe that a raped woman has demeaned the fam-ily and then punish her with expulsion, exile, and even ston-ing the victim to death instead of the rapist. Your fear-based, racist religions become the chief residence of most of your delusional thinking, a thought process permeating every as-pect of public life, as if that insanity were sanity.

"We have two objectives in this manifestation to you: first to keep you from global self-destruction, even though you are ideologically and ecologically committing suicide. Secondly, to nurture you into the cosmos, a creation we all share throughout this galaxy and the external space-time continuum of all other exo-galactic systems.

4

"By no means are you ready or prepared for direct inter-stellar visitation or communication or a more integrated participation in the galaxy at this time. Therefore, necessity requires us to offer you some reasons why, reasons so ubiquitous that to enumerate them would be encyclopedic. We have chosen, instead, to communicate with you by this modest and tranquil means.

"Let's first attempt to show in this contact with each other we consider it a civil and appropriate one. When you encounter my people and those who are identified as being different from yourselves they must be treated with the utmost respect and dignity.

"Unfortunately, where contacts between earth people and mine have occurred, I have seen my people and others put in hand-cuffs, starved to death, or treated with barbaric, desultory, and damaging indifference, ultimately inflicting death and shooting down various aerial Extraterrestrial Vehicular Craft (EVCs), ours and others, with the usual and unnecessary loss of life. Taking our people in custody in a numinous 'unregistered' category by your military is a mockery for which reason EBE's must be treated with respect knowing that they will be placing their minds and bodies in a form that transcends common bloody conflicts of you humans.

"Until you know what is happening, our presence should be regarded as a threat. For those of us who live in poly-holographic worlds, we want you to evolve into the plastic interrelationships possible for you once you realize you are already holographic beings. The universe, God, if you will, make you and all of us that way.

"If we were a threat to your existence or well-being, whatever catastrophe you may envision now, would have occurred many thousands of years ago when our and other intergalactic communities visited this planet.

"Look at us with a kindly demeanor and not through the lenses of fear and false prophesies. Your past histories in terms of slavery, wonton brutality, mass murder, racism, and sexism, warped perceptions of the self, you do not understanding how profoundly and naturally good you are programmed to be, given your genetic and DNA makeup.

"How some of you mock the creation of the natural world in your celebration of self and non-self. Your survival mechanisms override your good judgment. You think you need to control everything and every thought of everyone and everything around you. It violates your native humanity, separates you from your fellow human beings and all of nature around you. What incredible arrogance you display, not unlike hairy gorillas pounding their chests."

> So, X, you print such a poor image of us. Why
> do you even want to talk to us and just fly on
> by?

"You may not welcome our presence here with you, nor is it a purely nurturing act on our part that brings us here. We are here out of necessity. Like an unruly child, the human genome is in need of repair. A little conceptual nudging will bring you no harm either. I have volunteered for this dialogue with you as a service to my fellow Aryans; and NO, before you start associating us with the Nazi claims of being heirs to a superior race of humans; Aryah is simply what we call our Planet of Origin (our PoO). Having made those introductory remarks, you may have some questions."

> My God! After that long explanation, what can
> I say?

Hesitatingly, I wanted to say something, but felt a little overwhelmed by X's long dissertation, mostly I was hoping X would not expect me to remember everything he, she, it was telling me. So, I typed a few polite and conciliatory words:

> Yes, of course, finally! I want to learn from you
> everything I can but why me? I am feeling a
> little worried. I guess I should be honored,
> maybe a little special but uncertain as to why.

"Well, no reason to feel special. You were chosen just because you are not. You are an average bloke representing the majority of humans (Terrans) on this third planet from the sun."

> That is very uplifting, thank you. Now I feel
> even more uncertain...crap.

"Good, an appropriately humble way for any Terran to start. You tend to process more when you are stressed and unhappy. Hang on. I will give you some clarity of the big picture in which you find yourselves. Clarity tends to bring peace of mind."

PASSING DELUSIONS
AND OTHERS THAT REMAIN

So, upon reading this preface, I decided to try out more communications, to see what I might reply on the keyboard. It's not prestidigitation, just a lot of questions and answers. I am thinking maybe this kind of thing is what the ancients called their 'muses' except this is no poetry or something that would seem to be 'divinely inspired.' So, I just started typing and asking a question:

Why are you talking to me?

"Because you asked me here."

I did? Well, here we go. You just said you have two objectives. So, how could I have called you? We are presumably communicating tele-pathically, you said. Am I correct in assuming you can tell what I am saying by watching what I type? I am just having thoughts and don't know if you are transmitting those thoughts or if I am inventing them myself."

"I cannot see your typing, nor do I care. I will call you TED."

Me? I do have a name. Yeah. Why that?

"Yes, *TED001*, translates as *Terrestrial Entity Delta, zero, zero, one*. I am calling you by that name because your personal name is not important, but this is registered in my memory as an identifying reference: Terrestrial Entity Delta stands for your existence as a terrestrial from the third mass from the sun; hence, the fourth letter of the Greek alphabet with a triangular letter *delta (Δ)*, TED for short."

Does the '001' mean I am the first TED you've conversed with?

"No. And that's not important either. Let's get to the point. We are wasting time. I will just call you 'TED'"

O.K. So, what should I call you?

"I have already told you. That's enough."

What do you look like?

"You really get ahead of yourself, don't you? First, you must understand, I do not need to read your typing as I am already reading your mind."

Of course, telepathy, I should have thought of that.

"Now to the question of why we are having this conversation."

I am looking forward to it, I think.

"Probably not! I think we have seen and are going to see more of what an undeveloped specie you are at this point in time, possibly even in a regressive state."

You mean a recession, don't you?

"No. A global regression occurs when the population of a planet begins to be afraid of everything and everyone and for the good reasons they created themselves. Most troubling, those who create and cause this regression tend to be in charge. First, I must inform you that as a specie you are rude, up-tight, living life in fear of all creatures of the planet and of the universe itself, but mostly of your fellow human beings and regarding the latter, not without good reason.

"When any earthly culture is threatened by the new or the unexplainable, you hang onto the familiar and old in a desperate way, as if to stop change itself. Sometimes you use ancient images, icons of a culture and racial identity to insure stability and certainty, as if they had a capacity to give you stability or certainty. Your basic problem is knowing how to process information without new information becoming destructive to your sense of well-being.

"Both fear and anxiety are based on poorly processed social delusions and having no idea of the basic and structures of your global social order. It is as if there is no such thing outside your own creation, beings that you are. You are the only creatures on this earth who create this dichotomy from what is tangibly, tacitly real, and what are both the gifts and terrors of your imaginations."

Are you talking to me? Are you talking to me about me, or about all of humanity?

"You sound confused, TED. Very simply, I am focusing on you, an American, and your nation-state (the United

States of America) as it is the most dominant at this time and the most emulated, for better or worse. In general, you earthlings are at a place in your history that is so dangerous and potentially so self-destructive that you recurrently find yourselves in a circular path for which reason we cannot allow you to share in the galactic community at this time."

What...

"We know why you live in constant dread and it is quite simple to understand, saturated as you are at all levels of images of death and unsorted random thoughts. You create monolithic fantasies so far-reaching and so often repeated over generations you cannot recognize when something has run its course or when something quite new and remarkable has happened. Moreover, you are deathly afraid that if your culturally transmitted delusions, with all their associated delusional values are taken away, you will collapse socially and personally die. If those fantasies were to disappear, you believe you would be left with virtually nothing. Without your cultural rituals and inability to absorb and store information in your mind in a natural and calm way, you believe life would be groundless, a psychological void, as if you had suddenly lost a family member, or all order in the universe."

What do you mean you cannot allow us to be among you, in "the Galactic Community?"

"In-as-much as you have protected yourselves in this way for thousands of years you are, in fact, left with virtually nothing but fragile edifices of fantastic, unreal perceptions. In your agrarian and sun-worshipping religions of death and resurrection for thousands of years, earthlings have created concepts that can never be realized.

"You do have something, however. You have nature's gift in the form of this blue, water-based, hydrogen-oxygen planet and regardless of where you delusionally believe you came from. You do have life in all the complexity and beauty that time and the fabric of the universe have given you. For that we honor your presence among us, but for the previously stated reasons, we cannot allow you to join an immeasurably greater experience and begin to share in a healthier and sane cosmic childhood until some corrections and mental growth occurs."

> X, I don't see what is so terribly bad about us since what is out there in space scares us half to death. That seems pretty 'natural.' But now you have given me a new concern. Why are we so unworthy of a cosmic connection? I feel like I am being interviewed for admission into a fraternity.

"In your own misguided way you have asked me two questions, not one, although you see them as related. I will address the first and save the latter for later.

"Your civilization, as you call it, is dead, finished, done! You have unintentionally and unknowingly entered into the holographics of a polyholographic universe, an awareness of a greater interconnectedness from the tiniest physical particle/energy forms to the greater cosmos."

I replied to X right away:

> You don't mind being blunt. Why do you say that? Civilization on earth is obviously not dead.

"You cannot recognize this fact because you are still breathing. Even though your war-making and means of total destruction are vast, ever present, and trigger-ready you think you are safe. You psychologically project and acquire all the things and wealth you can as symbols of control. You use these ephemeral objects as a means for claiming meaningfulness, in spite of the void they ultimately represent, leaving you to grab for whatever cultural promise of certainty you can.

"In the meantime, thinking you deserve it all by some divine right, you create the greatest dangers to survival of not only Americans or human beings in general, but all that sustains you in nature as human beings.

"In your country you enjoy a modicum of health and well-being which the rest of the planet's people think is the great purpose in which everyone should participate or attempt to emulate, when in fact you have one of the most ineffective health systems on the planet and a tyrannical and brutalizing financial system.

"You rate 68th among the industrial countries in deaths of newborns. Does that speak well of your health system? It is the most expensive and least effective among all industrial nations having health concerns. Through your self-centered focus, all appears well, even though millions of human beings like yourself have growing doubts about you. Millions more on this planet are actually dying each day from starvation. An estimated 44,000 children die per day globally from militarism, lack of medical knowledge, absence of the simplest technologies or access to them, food, and clean water. An estimated 17 to 20 American veterans of your wars commit suicide daily. Three of five children in the U.S. are under fed or fed poorly in terms of nutrition.

"People are dying from pure ignorance, to say nothing of the inherent compassion, altruism, and love most humans on the planet are blessed with to one degree or another. Just the same, thousands die daily because of nationalistic, self-aggrandizing delusions you in your country and all other nation states, hold. These self-delusions reveal their duplicity especially in wars of revenge and violent struggles for industrial resources."

> Wait, we can't help it if we have developed better legal systems, better technologies, better economic practices in Europe, Japan, and my country than people in other parts of the world. Why do you say civilization is dead anyway, especially when you just said we have a modicum of health and well-being?

"Just for those very reasons, TED001. Look up 'modicum.' These are all part of your self-delusion, your oblate egotism, greed, and quest for 'power over.'"

> This is beginning to make me angry!

"There, you just dipped into your ego, your wounded self. It is deep and completely artificially induced."

> What do you mean 'Power Over'? Don't you mean domination?

"When you were born, you were born joyous and happy providing your mother was not poisoning herself or being abused by your modern obstetric nonsense. What happened to your innocent happiness? I want to answer my own question before you interject something ridiculous again."

"Against all odds, some of your species remain happy and joyous throughout their lives either because they became totally sucked into their inherited and own personally adopted delusions, which include bodyguards of denials, or because they were born and raised in a way that made it impossible to be otherwise. Wouldn't you agree to that?"

Actually, I wouldn't agree. I really don't know anyone born happy and stayed that way. I was happy until I was about ten or eleven. As I got older, murders, man-caused accidents, natural disasters, genocide, threats of nuclear war, poverty, the tax man, politicians, officious busybodies, and brainless fuddy duddies of all ages keep trying to control my every move and thought that might have intruded on my life. No, I don't think many keep experiencing happiness or even well-being for very long even if they were born that way. Sooner or later, something bad happens. When that happens, people lose their delusions.

"TED! No, listen to your thought process. People do not lose their delusions, nor any of those infinitely twisted obfuscations meant to mask their delusions. Delusions are implanted in all your youth by well-meaning parents and teachers and the general social order, whose own delusions were installed culturally.

"Worse, once a range of culturally accepted delusions are implanted, any other delusion is considered anathema and blasphemous. Humans not only hang onto the ones they have more dearly and more tightly desperately attempting to use delusions to alleviate psychic pain. "Regrettably, you invent new ones, piling them higher and woven more deeply into the fabric of personal and collective memories."

Wow. That's pretty damning.

"More often than not, your fellow humans go to their graves with this mental garbage. You kill your fellow human beings for and by the sanctions of your delusions. You create and mastermind endless suffering for yourselves and every living thing on the planet consciously and unconsciously. A good portion of it the result of poor infant nurturing, the rest by no educating humans on what you most need to know."

You are saying humans are inherently bad, then?

"Of course not! I will inform you about the importance of motherhood and nurture later. To answer your question: Emphatically no. I am saying you have the potential for enormous good and joy. It is shown in some way in almost everyone's behavior at one time or another. It's planted in your DNA, the shape and functions of your yet fully undeveloped mind and little used brain. That goodness is embedded in all life throughout the universe Few of earth's people have ever achieved a life of well-being and happiness, as we will see, hindered by the self-regulating delusions and unprocessed information you are constantly encountering."

How can you say our civilization, human civilization, is dead?

"Mainly, I can declare that because I am not deluding myself about you humans or your history. All of your major institutions are simply failing and not transiting out of the last or latest delusional cycle. What that means is that you have reached a horizon where you are gradually encountering so many delusional cycles that you are slowly awakening to an awareness your entire mythical structure is collapsing"

What do you mean 'delusional cycle' 'mythical structure?'

"I am referring to what you call 'periods' in history. These are very common cycles in early human development. When someone who sees too man things wrong, he or she is often attacked, excoriated, and often killed in the name of righteousness and deity.

I hope that your knowledge of galactic history shows we are not that different from the evolution of other earth-based intelligences.

14

"Didn't you hear my last sentence? We have intervened in human development from time to time, but our directive is to leave other species alone unless honorable contact can be made or until a situation has become critical, as in your case. By the way, just for clarity, Kardashev's Scale, which attempts to classify intelligent galactic world types into three basic levels of technological development, is quite fallacious. At least it is an attempt to think beyond a delusional political history based on successions of kings and queens, military conquests, and religious–economic imperialism."

What do you mean by honorable contact?

"I mean that the visitee, meaning you in this case, try not to kill us just because we look different, transport ourselves in different vehicles, and for good reason, are reluctant to communicate. Instead, you should welcome us with greetings rather than fear and despair. At least show a little humility. Don't put our numerous species you have captured in interrogation rooms, in hand-cuffs, or treat them with any less dignity you would any foreign dignitary or traveler. If the many galactic entities (GE's) that have escaped the gravity of their home planets and have the technology to fly interstellar spaces in times exceeding the speed of light, we, and others, could easily dispose of all human beings to make room for ourselves if we so wished. Fortunately for you, most of us are advanced well beyond that kind of imperious grabbing of 'Living Space, *lebens raum*,' as Adolf Hilter called it."

I don't think anything like that has happened.
Where ET's were put in handcuffs and interrogated?

"It has happened. Both have happened."
Oh Boy, I'm confused. What both?

"Both genocide in the name of making land available to what was perceived by delusional people who considered themselves superior, who called their land victims "savages" and many other pejorative, mendacious names they wished. Your Euro-Anglo treatment of native peoples, was committed by the cultural delusion of superiority and land-grabbing, leading to genocide, in the name of that delusion.

"Here is the point. Your military have leaked certain photos to soften the shock they expect humans will otherwise feel when they realize there is life outside their own planet and solar system and the most intelligent are not necessarily the prettiest. You still revert to your lizard brain when anything contrary to your limited experience and knowledge shows itself. It's a defense mechanism of the oldest part of your brain, over which you will eventually transcend. If you do not, you will perish and the earth with you."

The think next thing you are going to tell me
that Jesus was actually one of yours.

"Not quite! Well, He was not one of Ours. You have a hard time keeping focused on a linear train of thought, don't you? O.K., Jesus' message was very human, but it was one so profound that most humans could not embrace it, dangling all kinds of senseless artifacts in the face of what might be gleaned from the extensive revisions of his teachings."

So, you do not believe what Jesus said has actually reached us except in a greatly modified form?

"No, of course not. Your Thomas Jefferson rewrote the New Testament, taking out all of the fantasies about Jesus, the miracles, the virgin birth, and transcendental nonsense in an attempt to identify what Jesus was really like. He succeeded where the innumerable revisionists translated the event of his death over millennia as something absolutely phantasmagoric, thinking in metaphors, as was as common at that time as were Roman crucifixions."

So, what is that, a delusion too? You mean the Resurrection from the dead?

"*Post-mortem*, Jesus was very quickly turned into an agricultural resurrection deity, sharing that title with over thirty-three other resurrection gods in the ancient world-- those are gods who die, resuscitate (resurrect), and ultimately ascend into paradise and return to the stars. It is an ancient formula for changes in earth's seasons and the daily death and rebirth of the sun.

The founders and subsequent followers of the deified man-god syncretically merged Jesus' story into something that the masses of ancient Mediterranean society would have easily understood and believe because of the existence of these many other resurrection deities. Only modern religions find it unique because of their ignorance of human history with the emergence of city states translated into a delusional formula for human life reinforced by an agrarian understanding about life."

Isn't the idea of eternal life more a solution humans make to explain and liberate themselves from the apparent absoluteness of death?

"The need for resurrection deities is just as closely bound to agricultural societies as fertility gods and goddesses and the sun 'dying every day and resurrecting the next unless sometime terrible has happened; namely an apocalypse, a death of the world. As for the issue of the denial of one's personal mortality, I will explain that to you later, just to say now you have difficulty processing human mortality. In the meantime, I need to help you out of your domestic and global delusions. May I continue?"

Yes, of course, although I do not think I am going to like it.

"Delusions and illusions are nearly the same, a witch's brew of illusions, optical, mental, luminary, creations of mind-sets, creations of mind, faulty memory with composite fragments of actual and testable information. For example, if you see three-masted sailing ship on the horizon above a desert sand dune or highway created by heat waves, you recognize it as an illusion of light refracted through multiple lenses provided by the heat of something that might look like a sailing ship. On the other hand, you know such craft do exist. Delusions are more a mental state of a hypothesized reality. The 'ships' of your reality are delusions, mostly symbolic psychological defenses against everything you do not understand or accept as real or valid."

O.K. I'm not sure what you mean. What do you mean about 'accept?' But please continue.

"For short, your most serious unacceptable is the finality of organic death of the human body. In that regard, collective and self-imposed delusions are the source of most of human suffering and death. For example, politicians and many citizens of your country say you live in a democracy. When challenged they will admit it might be more like a republic, but it is neither of these. Democracy is a socio-political delusion based on fragmentary evidence and a willfully hypothesized reality you wish to be true because of another delusion that 'Democracy is good,' at least better that its opposite, tyranny.

"A secondary delusion emerges from the first based on other fantasies, fears, and symbolic or magical thoughts; namely, that people who support a democracy are therefore good or less confused than people without such a political system and are therefore better people."

I think you are going to explain this further, right?

"For now it is important only to embrace the concept that every delusion gives birth to a cascade of infinitely more delusions, all cross-referencing each other and reinforcing each other as 'proofs' on a grandiose scale."

"This cascade and each delusional descent is so interwoven with your thought processes that you come quickly to believe, as a child, that if any one of your delusions is exposed for the fantasy that it really is, your society, country, social or religion group, family, and even your own personal psyche will just fall apart. With such changes, you fear life itself will be destroyed. To put it in terms of one of your favorite preoccupations, 'explosions,' real and not, you fear reality would come as an explosion of human social structure that would seemingly disintegrate everything."

Yes, well it's for that reason that the U.S. military is keeping information about EBE's top secret, in fear that contact will destroy all current religious beliefs and create psychological, financial, and social chaos. They're afraid that for conservative religious people, such a revelation will be very hard.

"Historical Terran events would say they are right. However, if such delusional systems were to collapse, you would not die but find a new life energy no longer being drained by the requirements and burdens of the delusions. If your want to look at what happened to aboriginal peoples throughout the Americas, Africa, and the South Pacific, it would look like the hiding of Alien contact in secrecy be necessary. Without their tribal delusions and externally imposed Christianism or Muslim ideologies, some individual native peoples, even whole communities withered and died, that is, if they were not murdered outright when enforced coercion did not work.

"'Primitives' and 'savages,' as they were called by Europeans and other invading groups--enforced by right-thinking missionaries, merchant men, and pirates for the 'savages' to adopt the languages and customs of the conquerors. They were coerced into abandoning their time-honored customs, dress, and cultural delusions, sold into slavery or treated as savages, barbarians, sub-humans or non-humans, 'aliens.' Those who simply could not make that transition died, others succeeded over time to adjust in some degree to newly imposed standards. After several generations, the old delusions die out, most traditions are forgotten by survivors and lose their meaning because of endless adaptations. Those earlier indigenous traditions are outright forbidden by the masters of the new order. Often the conquistadors to be demand old traditions be less used or considered evil. It's called 'conquest.'"

Yes, that is what we are afraid of, when the extraterrestrials make themselves known and governments admit their presence, they will conquer us. Maybe even eat us.

"Fear Again! You can continue those traditions based on practical and enjoyable activities be they, reading, culinary traditions, costume, helping others, as long as they are not based on magical acts intended to manipulate and create miraculous results. Who would pray for an architectural form? I ask you, once constructed, does its shape, textures, or fascination become diminished? Is it enhanced by magical sayings, adornment with icons and blessed with holy water?

"Your inner Self works the same way. It is another measure of your place and being in the universe. If an ostensibly miracle occurs, accept that something is happening that you do not yet understand. Don't assume some magical, unseen, good or evil entity caused it.

"In California a plane crashed in San Diego killing all on board. A Catholic nun who arrived too late to board the plane proclaimed '*God saved me.*' I guess her God forgot about all the other people who died. "

LOG III

DELUSIONS AND ANCIENT METAPHORS

X, we all know America is not exactly a true democracy. So, I don't think it is completely a delusion. The word comes from humankind's first experience with a democracy in ancient Athens. It means authority or power of the people in Greek (*demos kratia*) where people elected their officials.

Plato refers to it by another name, a republic, which in Latin (*res publica*) just means 'things of the people.' So both titles mean essentially the same thing. Plato didn't like either name given to it and attempted to prove its inherent failures. Since I haven't read *The Republic*, I don't know why he so objected to a democracy or republic.

"As well he should, TED!"

Should what, why?

"Plato was attempting to rid himself and his followers of delusions, to seek greater values, like honesty and truth. But, you did it again, TED. You refer to humankind? 'Humankind,' implies a kindly humanity, does it not? It could be just another delusion embedded in your day-to-day language like most of your delusions. Everything humans think of as society or culture is really a semantic creation. Keeping those words in mind, let's continue with your self-imposed delusions, the most obvious being your assumption that you live in a 'civilization.'"

Oh, great, not only is my democracy a delusion, but we're going to see how civilization itself is a delusion!

"This is no time for intellectual cowardice. Instantly, we find ourselves coping with an embedded belief or delusion about the word 'civilization.' It derives from *civis*, a Latin word just referring to city. It is another arbitrary delusion of

21

your ancient world where a dichotomy exists between city dwellers and country people. From the earliest days, those living in towns and cities viewed themselves, as in Athens and elsewhere, as being superior to those who were not."

People still do! If you live in California or L.A. and come to New York City, even the busboys and taxi drivers who speak mostly Russian think you are from the crazy part of the country. It's the same in Paris, London, and Berlin.

"Do not miss my point. A 'citizen' is a construct, a hypothesized reality assuming one's basic intelligence and intrinsic personal worth more valuable than that of rural and mountain people on whom they deeply depended for food and utilitarian materials.

"By mythologizing these polarities the Greeks personify the city folk as physically ideal, in contrast to the illiterate country and mountain folk in the form of Centaurs, creatures with half-human, half-horse bodies. These biomorphic adaptations contrast the 'civilized' Lapiths as physically and socially ideal citizens creating a *meme*, as one of your authors has called it. This *meme* or embedded memory theme is really another delusion creating class and racial elitisms."

I need to quickly interject that, America, I mean the U.S., has been having many triumphs over racism and social biases, as with Blacks, women, and gays.

"You get a little excited don't you TED?"

Ah. Well, it's not every day I talk with an ET.

"Back to your ancient Greeks, please! To their credit that polarity between the mythological Lapith and Centaur also served another metaphor about the duality of human nature.

"Finding himself in an internal psychic conflict with his base humanity, coerced largely by his sexual drives, the ancient Greek captures in this myth an enjoyable story for children, who might take it literally, but also for an adult who might recognize there is more to it.

"Not only were the Lapiths city dwellers and therefore 'civilized' beings in contrast to the half-human, half-horse people of the craggy mountains, who were rough, ignorant, and uncouth, but who nevertheless live in a kind of peaceful co-existence. Once, during a more peaceful time the Lapiths invited the Centaurs to a wedding of a young Lapith couple. The ceremony went well initially. The bride was beautiful, her husband strong and athletic but after the Centaurs drank too much wine, they attempted to abduct the bride and other women, precipitating a great battle in which Hercules himself had to come to the aid of the Lapiths.

"In contrast to the Lapith perceptions of a city dweller to think and act rationally, the people of the countryside were in stark contrast. Educated people of the city and its fluid exchange of ideas provides an insight, a story about the internal conflict between the two internal natures of man. One is his capacity for rationality, based on human reason and the other, the nature of his animal passions arising from human sexuality and his capacity for passionate emotions, warfare, a disparity the ancient Greeks were honest enough to face in the metaphor of the Centaur."

So, if I understand you correctly, the half-man, half-horse Centaurs symbolized the untamed animal part of human beings, and the rational thinking Lapiths or city dwellers, who thought on a higher, more noble level were able to control those passions by means of their capacity to reason. Right?

"More or less! Let's leave out "higher," and "level" for reasons I will explain, as it is one of the linguistic *memes* that locks you into mental slavery to hierarchy. Other Greek myths performed similar functions. Again this arbitrary differentiation of class reinforces partial truths, imagined truths and their interlocking rationales all supporting their multiple delusions about themselves and others, be they rural people, Persians, or people from the next town."

That was a long time ago X. We don't even think that way anymore. Yes, I remember the stories of the Lapiths and Centaurs appearing in carved marble on Greek temples, but we don't do that any longer. We don't think in metaphors or carve them on buildings.

"Too quick to answer again, TED. Look, you know that on any Washington D.C. buildings there may be sculptures, paintings, phrases, and symbols that are both literal and allegorical. You find ubiquitous examples throughout Vertical Societies. What would you say about the modern iconographies on church walls, sculptures, and priestly garments, bejeweled crowns and croziers of the Roman Catholic and Eastern Orthodox churches? By contrast Mohammed, traveling over the peripheries of the East Roman empire came in contact with iconoclastic monks who lived in desert villages and caves, refusing images of any kind. It also in contact with Jews from whom he literally interpreted the Mosaic first commandment '*Thou shalt have no other Gods before me,*' forbidding the making of humanoid images. On the one hand he spared the tribal people of his own land the multiple level interpretations of historic and extraordinary events expected and sought in the Greco-Roman world, but on the other, his Muslim followers were constrained from developing a narrative tradition which, otherwise, existed in rich abundance in all other parts of the world.

Islamists do tend to be literalists.

"Not correct and not the point! Everywhere on your planet people take everything as a children's story in a purely literal sense. Hence, the delusions you live by are seen as actual, true, and fact. For example, Great Britain, the Netherlands, and Sweden, and many more very modern countries still have kings and queens. Just look at the pomp and pretentious ceremony displayed by the British, a people who consider themselves the home of modern science and rational thinking, a country identified with 18th century citizens like Locke, Hume, Newton, and Bacon.

"These social, political, and religious events and ceremonies are your temples differ only in the iconographies from those of your ancient ancestors. Delusional values are what you call culture. Culture and its study has become the very thing that prevents you and millions of others from participating in a real world with equal opportunity. You are passing into but not yet participating in your future."

24

You don't understand, X. We have equal opportunity. Again, Thomas Jefferson: '*All men
are created equal...*'

"Stop, please, these interjections! To summarize: you
agreed that there might be some delusional thinking and I
gave it to you as the chief reason you cannot yet be admitted
to the galactic community."

O.K., I accept that, although I feel deeply troubled by it.

"Secondly, we learned from just one ancient myth that
the Greeks were at least conscious that they had two natures,
one animal and passionate and one logical with a capability
of being rational. As uncomfortable as they might seem, these
are two conditions, which separate your world from the galactic community, is also one that separates you from yourself
and from the beautiful environment that gave birth to you on
this 'pale blue planet,'"

Yes, I agree. Not only that, modern neurologi-
cal science has shown that the right and left
hemispheres of the frontal lobes of the human
brain tend to lean in one or the other of those
two directions, passion vs. reason, on the right
hemisphere and left, respectively.

"A great over-simplification, TED, but close enough. I
must take you next to the most severe delusion that you Terrans have carried from ancient times into the present, which
has been and will continue to be the most irrational and destructive delusion in human history. It is a disease worse than
a plague and covers the earth in many guises."

THREE SURVIVAL GEOMETRIES OF MAN

"Be at peace TED, I am not attacking you, just trying to open some 'doors of perception,' as Aldous Huxley once put it, without the necessity of mescaline or other drugs.

"One of the assets discovered by other GE's is that early in our many histories we learned to find truths in geometric form. We speak and write with geometric forms, the most sophisticated one, the torus, which opens the universe, but you are not ready for that. Plato and Greeks like Pythagoras and Euclid got a stumbling start on it, as did for other Greeks, even though they most likely received everything they knew and recorded from the ancient Egyptians at a time when Egypt was in a general state of collapse.

"What I am going to tell you is much more simple and intelligible, given that you already know something about your world history from anthropology, archeology, and sociology."

Thanks, I am grateful you appreciate I know something.

"The Primary Concept is this: All geometries I am about to use, describe survival mechanisms. Geometries are among the first thought images that attempt to control the world by establishing boundaries. It might be an ocean or lake boundary, boundaries of desert, of weather, vegetation, mountain ranges, most of all the geometries of North, South, East and West, and the list goes on. Geometries also provide infinite boundaries and structures of solar and galactic dimensions as many GE's have demonstrated in crop circles impressed in the crops of farmlands all over your planet. So, while geometry is controlled boundary-making, it is a gateway to understanding the boundaries of the universe."

Good. I want to hear more about that. I was wondering when we would get to more subjects of outer space. Do those boundaries in space mean they are claimed by different groups like the 'Klingon's?"

"No. TEΔ001, don't you see how you take an analogy from one utterly unrelated thing to another?"

"Very well then, to continue. As a human species, you are identified as *Homo sapiens,* who emerge only about 90,000 to 100,000 earth years ago, distinct from Cro-Magnons and Neanderthals."

They came in the order I cited them. Okay, most people know that. Although I'm not sure which came first.

"*Homo* (man) emerges from unconsciousness to a sentient awareness as an upright, bipedal hominid. Your official terminology *homo sapiens* here means "man who thinks" The second *sapiens* added implies that at this stage he is thinking still better. We prefer to call *homo sapiens sapiens* "man who thinks he thinks.""

Did you just make a joke?

"In your earliest primitive social order, you lived in a primal Planar world. As he wanders over the plane, the 'horizontal' surface of the planet, foraging and hunting for food, *homo sapiens sapiens* learns which plants can be eaten safely, which can be manipulated for shelter, which animals are a threat and some to be killed and eaten, others domesticated."

Why this lesson in stone-age history? I thought we were going to start talking about 'space.'

"We are! Your historical inner space! For your early Planar ancestors there is the sky above and the plane of the earth below. His world is migratory, hunting and gathering on what appears as that horizontal and two-dimensional plane of the earth, creating in his mind a flat map of the earth and sky, which appears two-dimensional and Planar to him. His space is what is above and what is below and distances."

O.K. That makes sense but where are you going with this because you just described three directions and therefore three dimensionality?

"Confused by his own ego, and his own movements over the plane of the earth and becomes confused by all of the movements of both earth and sky until one day he stays in a place long enough to think of the earth as a variegated but stable surface plane and the sky as a moving vault above. Moving day and night, the nomadic sky turns with an order he thought only existed on the Plane of the earth bound between mountains, valleys, rivers and caves, oceans, and with their respective vegetation and local animal life."

But X, they are still moving in a three-dimensional space.

"Obviously, the nomadic hunter-gatherer would refer to this level of his reality as a horizontal surface, in spite of the variations in height and depth. This early phase of human thought processes we can identify as Planar Society. In certain parts of Terra there are whole societies maintaining a near facsimile of life as it once existed in those primordial times. Life is free, abundant, fragile, and often deadly.

"Your myth of the hero cowboy is part of that attempt at reverting to a more 'down-to-earth' and 'free' life, a mythology just the same. This migratory Planar culture survived for thousands of years, including the so-called 'Stone-Age' European cultures until they realized they were living on a sphere they might circumnavigate. Tribal groups of the "Old Stone Age" spread all over the planet, leaving little behind as a testimony to their existence. Occasionally, their need to make visual replications of animals, what you might call art, was primarily motivated by Magical Thinking."

Yes, X, of course I am aware of this time in human history. It is normally called the Paleolithic Period, usually said to begin around 37,000 years ago. The painted cave and rock shelters in France, Spain and other parts of central Europe date from this time, I think ending only around 11,000 BCE.

"How very academic. Everything you just plotted out is true, but painfully inadequate to those of us who know a more precise dating and history of the early human experience, which I shall not go into. Suffice it to say, TED, that when the great ice melts occurred around 14,000 years ago, the human mind had developed to the extent that it attempted to take control of its newly unsettled environment, it created Logical Analogies."

What do you mean '*Logical analogies*?' That sounds kind of sophisticated for a bunch of cavemen. And I thought you just said they did Magical Thinking.

"They weren't cavemen. They were people just like you, thinking, conscious, self-aware human beings. Only their technology was primitive and their thoughts concerning their relationship to the animals and their migrations, the coming and going of seasons, of the availability of different kinds of food during some seasonal cycles not available at others.

"Before I proceed any further, do you understand what I mean about the pre-civilized man as being a part of a Planar society?"

No, not really.

"Good. Do you understand the symbolic geometry of the plane and what the relationship of man to plane is all about?"

Well, it sure doesn't seem to have anything to do with geometry, but I am beginning to see why you want to use abstract terminologies.

"Only on a level of abstraction does the geometry of a Planar society serve as a metaphor for a social survival concept."

So you are equating it with survival. That makes more sense.

"Clearly, you do not understand, but we will come back to it later and it will appear more reasonable to you. In the meantime, let me elaborate on the Planar world, what you also call the Paleolithic period, or Old Stone Age."

Yes, please. That will probably help.

"When you mentioned 'cavemen,' you were probably thinking of the painted caves found throughout southern France and Altamira Spain."

Yes, it is a logical deduction, since it is the only
area where such paintings survive.

"True, a deduction it is but the only problem with that is Paleolithic man did not live in those caves he painted. There is only evidence of fires briefly burned and then abandoned, meaning they used those caves to paint images in them and that's it. These caverns were treated as magical places where someone you might equate with a shaman or sage could paint cows, horses, large hunting cats, woolly mammoths and other animals of the hunt (many of which no longer live in southern France, some, like the woolly mammoth, rhinos, and large cats), most of which have long been extinct in those parts of the northern hemisphere."

I know those animal depictions are pretty sophisticated in their representation, I mean so
naturalistically done that they are recogniza-
ble to anyone today. I have heard that the
painters (you call them shamans) even took
into account the shapes of the vault of the
caves to emphasize projecting muscles around
the animals shoulders and hind quarters,
which made them even more realistic. So,
what is so Planar about that?

"Again, Planar is just an abstract geometric description of a social means of survival."

And you claim that there is evidence of planar-
ity and/or survival exhibited in these paintings, naturalistic ones at that?

"Oh, my goodness. Yes, in at least five major ways. First, images are almost always captured by a containing outline that encloses the animal's silhouette, a two-dimensional en-closing line. Second, there is an absence of a setting or any kind of environment, not even a ground line on which the an-imal in a three-dimensional world would stand. No ground lines appear beneath any animal in any representation of the Paleolithic era to indicate identification with the solid ground, with the earth. Third, there are no representations of the hunters, except in one case, located in the lower cave at Lascaux. Even there the humanoid figure is dying, screaming in agonizing pain having been gored by a disemboweled raging bull standing in the space above him. Fourth, in many of the caves the painted and sculpted animals have been struck by actual spears, axes, and arrow heads. In one case a horse, more like a pony, hand-sculpted in clay in the cave at Lascaux has been beaten to death by round clubs. Holes indenting the entire body were made while the clay was still soft, testifying the animal in the floor of the cave was symbolically 'killed.'

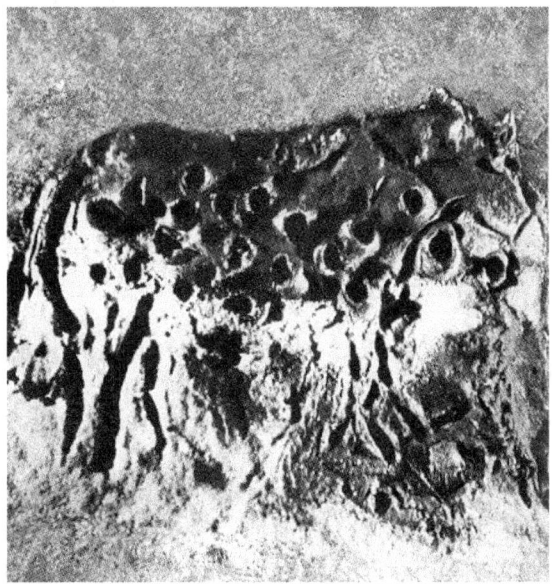

Figure 1. "Killed Horse," A clay figure found on the floor of the cave. (ca. 40-15,000 BCE). Unknown location, France. Photo: unknown source. See *Encyclopedia of World Art*, NY (1966), I, pls. 242-280.

"What this and other instances like it suggest is that the images are magical captures of the spirit or *anima*, the life force of the animal about to be hunted. Once ceremonially 'killed,' the hunters, braver in the delusion of their magical 'kill,' could expect less fear and success in the forthcoming hunt."

Yes, I once saw that image in an encyclopedia and thought that the artist just didn't like his

work, or maybe his tribe didn't and clubbed it
with dozens of blows.

"The 'killing' of an image of an animal is itself a fifth kind of two-dimensionality. Even though the animals of that kind are very realistic, three-dimensional, and potentially dangerous, any such 'killing' is a magical thought process, Magical Thinking is always two-dimensional concept, much like an on off switch. For example, 'I'm afraid,' 'I attack and kill a spirit image; now I'm not afraid.' Magical Thinking, so essential to Planar Society migrated into the subsequent Vertical Society without realizing its origins in Paleolithic/Planar cultures."

In modern psychology, when this kind of 'killing' or harming an animal or human is usually called 'sympathetic magic,' as with voodoo and similar practices. But what's Vertical Society?

"Vertical Society represents is the opposite human stage of survival thinking from a Planar, two-dimensional, hunter and gatherer society."

You mean Planar society is the same as Horizontal society?

"Not precisely, although I use the term inter changeably. It is another way of putting it, but too easily confused with a flatter or lateralized Vertical Society. People often believe that a Democracy is a Horizontal society, but since it is fixed on Place, providing an axis around which its domain ranges over.

So, even if a thought process like Voodoo or sympathetic magic is practiced in a Vertical Society, it is still not a Planar one nor is it horizontal.

"Yes, if sympathetic is a term you like to use. It represents neither sympathy nor empathy, but a magical practice dating at least from Paleolithic times for securing food through the hunt by making a soul image. It is the soul image captured in the images of the animals of the hunt. They float in space without reference to time or place. "

These paintings are in caves. Besides the fact they had no canvases or tubes of pigment, why paint in caves?

"There is every reason to not go into caves, much less paint in them on walls and ceilings that were often well above the height of the painter-hunter on cave vaults bespeckled with roots, bats, insects, and moisture. These images survive probably because anything done in more accessible places, as in exposed rock shelters were defaced by later human visitors or have disappeared from natural causes.

"Another reason for choosing caves is that a cavern can be seen as symbolic of the womb of Mother Earth who gives birth to the animals and by extension, to life itself. The fact that animals are painted in caves is either to insure success in the hunt, or to celebrate in a mystical and even mythical way the triumph of the human over wildness and the dangers of nature while celebrating the seemingly endless renewal of life in plants and animals."

"There is another possibility as well; namely, the joy of triumph over the most terrifying of beasts. Much later in time, in celebrations by the Romans, they actually hunted animals turned loose in an arena, some to extinction. In the ceremonial hunt was a sign of the triumph of man over nature and the abundance of food under the presumed 'wise' 'divine' leadership of the Roman emperors, a clearly two-dimensional thought process, except it occurred in a Vertical Society."

So, two-dimensional thinking is Planar, just as Magical Thinking is two-dimensional, right?

But they can co-exist in a Vertical Society.

"Yes, you understand, at last. Magical thinking is two-dimensional because it establishes the outer-most boundaries of thinking. Magical thinking devises the limits beyond which it is considered either too dangerous to go, outright foolish, or even evil. For those who dare to go beyond two-dimensional thinking are often considered punishable by death. Now let's move on. There is much more that you might learn and understand."

Wait X. I need to understand something. You have used the term 'Vertical Society' several times now. Besides being a social structure

33

    that would be identified with a survival mech-
    anism, what does Vertical Society really
    mean?

"You are leaping ahead. Good. The geometric abstraction 'Vertical Society' is everything you call civilization, from
the earliest villages, towns, and to city states, to your national
entities. George Kubler, a Yale anthropologist in the 1960's
looking at Mayan culture made the suggestion that humans
first lived in a Plane or Planar, two-dimensional culture in
tribal wanderings over the plane of the earth pursuing animals of the hunt.

"As the first towns were built, humanity entered into its
present Vertical, or what you might call a Pyramidal phase. It
is there where you are now stuck, one foot in the old Vertical
phase and the toe of the other foot in the third social structure, a multi-integrated, Holographic one. It is what some
people are promising or predicting as the New Age."

    You're not speaking of the Age of Aquarius,
    right?

"No, not in a light year."

    I think that since the discovery and splitting of
    the atom, that the third stage must be the Nu-
    clear Age.

"Nuclear Age is one of several fitting but inadequate de-
scriptors. But we are looking solely at the second kind of social structure, the Vertical Society where human beings are
presently stuck with and cannot and in many cases do not
want to see or experience anything else.

"There was of course a transition from stone-Age
hunter-gatherer/Planar cultures to Vertical ones, corre-
sponding to your Neolithic Age. It occurs as humans found it
easier to survive by staying in one place over a period of time,
risking all of the benefits that pursuit of migrating animals,
picking seasonal plants and the option of flight when external
threats of any kind came.

"A tribal or ancestral community choosing to stay in one
place had to organize and prepare for a variety of conditions
that do not apply in a Planar nomadic, fight or flight structure. The key term here is Place."

When you make the shift from a nomadic existence to a sited social structure at a place, I can imagine the physical, psychological, and practical shifts that have to be made?

"So, TED, what do you think those might be?"

First there would have to be water nearby. Next there would have to be some kind of common shelter type architecture. I would think there would have to be many small animals that can be hunted or domesticated, plants, and fruit locally, or they would have to grow their own to sustain a community.

"Everything you mention is a valid description of Place. However, once the hunter-gatherer stays in one place, he does so because there are certain advantages, at least to that Place. It becomes the tribal home. It is a birth-place, a returning point and a common dwelling place. All of the passages humans experience in life occur in reference to that Place, chief among them, birth, passing into adulthood, sexual relations and marriage, child rearing, life-sustaining activities like farming and herding, defense against outside influences, than death, and burial.

"In the earliest datable locations three to perhaps several dozen in Turkey and the city of Jericho in ancient Palestine (now part of modern Jordan). In the case of the Turkish locations at Çatal Hüyük, Göbekli Tepe, dating appears inconsistent with the sequence of emergent Vertical Societies.

"As identification with Place occurs, animal husbandry and farming require modest architecture as that found at Çatal Hüyük. But the megalithic structures of Göbekli Tepe predate Çatal Hüyük by as much as three-thousand years. Göbekli Tepe had to have been the result of a lost but primitive Vertical civilization dating much earlier than the remnants once considered the earliest towns.

"Göbekli Tepe consists of partial excavations of as many as ten monumental single-layered circular stone structures dating as early as 12,500 CE and more sophisticated than the nearby Çatal Hüyük, which has seven layers of adjacent buildings. In all three instances (Turkey and Jericho), they were located in fertile grassy savannahs where grains of many kinds could be found, small animals and hunting cats, some as large as lions. It has been claimed by one author that the apparent human need for grassy lawns and parks dates back to the first villages in the grassy savannahs of what is now modern Turkey."

> Yes, a green lawn is something many people cannot do without, no matter how small the house or estate, or how arid the climate.

"That relationship of Place to survival mode, occurs both at Çatal Hüyük and Jericho. In the lowest and oldest level of Jericho, beneath 27 layers of buildings destroyed and rebuilt, a deceased family member was buried next to the family hearth. His head, stripped of organic material was re-surfaced in clay as a facsimile of the deceased parent. He was buried up to his neck in a fetal position."

> Sounds horrifically gruesome. They ate their meals next to a corpse?

"In such instances, a beloved grandparent could be 'sustained' magically by his location next to the family cooking hearth and even symbolically fed. Death, dining, and the promise of the continuation of life are part of human ceremonies right down to the present time. They are very much part of the symbolism of pagan Roman *agape* feasts and the Christian ritual of the Last Supper, and magical ceremonies based on logical analogies that become social imprints of Magical Thinking referred to as 'masses' a word that has multiple meanings. In the Roman mass the word is associated with 'dismissal,' a word spoken by the priest at the end of the mass. But orally *messa* sounds like *mesa*, or table, and the administration of the Eucharist, a symbolic meal offered to the Faithful. It is around the hearth and ultimately the table where life-sustaining food is served, which reinforces the centrality of Place, in the home and overtime in the social community.

"Gordon Childe recognized this transitional phase of village building as a 'Barbaric phase,' another diminutive and unfortunate term. It was in this Transition phase that domestication of cattle, sheep, goats, dogs and other small animals occurred along with the appearance of baking ovens, decorative ornaments in gold and stone, and beer. In experimental villages over the centuries, traditions of story-telling, art and crafts were developed, essential to the full-blown vertical society which you call civilization.

"Civilization (Vertical culture) is an accumulation of complex hierarchies of authority with a supreme authority based on a single individual making the shift from *pater familias* the father as the head of the family to *pater patriae*, the father of his country as later celebrated by the Romans."

Yes, like George Washington, who is seen as a *pater patriae* after the Roman model. Horatio Greenough carved an image of him half-naked, enthroned as a Greco-Roman god, something that was done well after Washington had died, or the 'father of the country' might have done something in disgust to Horatio.

So, besides a few heroes, there are strata, positions within the Vertical hierarchy we would associate with status. Is that right?

"True, but to continue with the sequence: with the appearance of writing, words, fact, ideas could be recorded but Vertical cultures ultimately die, once cast, promising constancy and repeatability. Signs, letters, and symbols became measures of one's position in the Vertical strata. These became more important as the techniques of symbolic writing and other technological skills make possible a new class of laborers identified today in Vertical hierarchical-speak as a 'middle class.'

"Among the earliest Sumerian records (the earliest Mesopotamian city state) in cuneiform letters pressed into clay tablets, the vast majority are for business transactions, trading materials for animals, for land, and the like. Thousands of fragments were also found containing the legend of the hero king Gilgamesh, representing a new level of thinking combining common cultural moral and life-changing events. Gilgamesh, for example, though king of Sumeria, is altogether human, struggling with the temporaneity of human life after his best friend is killed by a lion on one of their hunts together."

So, when does the idea come about that a king or leader who is not only a hero and king, but a divine being?

"That notion of divine kingship is in direct response to the priority of importance as a definition of Vertical space around a sacred Place. The palace of the king and the main shrine of the gods are necessarily merged, placed on the highest hill or artificial hill (*tel*, or mound). It first appears in the city-state of Akkad, the immediate successor to Sumerian society, located north of Sumeria and farther inland. With the deification of their king Gudea as having divine attributes he becomes more than a hero like the Sumerian Gilgamesh. Gudea, the 'Patesi of Lagash' (Telloh, Iraq) appears to be the first in Mesopotamia to be considered part human and part god. With it, art forms shift from narrative to icon, from a kind of open form to a rigid compactness, where likeliness is subordinated to symbol.

http://www.louvre.fr/en/oeuvre-notices/gudea-prince-lagash-seated-statue-dedicated-god-ningishzida

"Now, rather than a hero, he is celebrated for water management by redirecting the river waters of the Tigris and Euphrates into 'the lands between the two rivers' (the Greek word 'Mesopotamia') to manage the annual floods and to provide water to numerous villages and farms. It was his genius that makes him a god, someone separate from and superior to ordinary human beings."

When I think about it, most deities are celebrated for some kind of ingenuity, energy, or gifts of genius or wisdom.

"Precisely, this is where the real tragedy of civilization, namely, Vertical Society occurs. It is where psychological separation occurs in a Vertical Hierarchy. Community ceases to be familial, ancestral, tribally oriented, but constructed on abstractions of hierarchy, including broad racial classifications. Even the use of the Greek term hierarchy makes this separation explicit, deriving from *hieros*, 'holy,' and *archos*,

38

the 'power of old men' or simply 'power.' A hierarchy is nothing less than '*Holy Power.*'

"In Vertical Society it is understood, if not always rationally, there exists always, in all things, a hierarchic order of authority that must be maintained for the city state and city centeredness ('civilization') to endure. If you become wealthy or powerful, it is proof that the gods have dispensed inherent greatness upon you and often to your family. It pushes you toward the apex of hierarchy. Therefore, it follows you are blessed by the supreme deities or deity in a way not available to most everyone else."

These ideas exist to this day.

"Albert Einstein recognized this separation humans feel about their fellow human beings and from the environment as one of the unfortunate qualities of humanity. It is not an inherent quality, however, even though those on the upper strata of hierarchical society consider it is."

It's amazing to me how much the concept and imagery of hierarchy is embedded in our language. We always speak in terms of higher vs. lower, in contrast to upper and lower class.

An employee may want a 'higher' wage; a wealthy person does not live among the lower [income] classes. All military organizations are hierarchical even to the point where a superior officer, like any 'superior' is always considered correct, leading to human catastrophes on unthinkable scales.

There is even an underclass and an underground, each referring the lowest form of survival and class. I can see how difficult it is to conceive and implement any kind of truly democratic institution in a Vertical Society, even though we talk a lot about 'Freedom' and 'Democracy.'

"Now you get it. Vertical Society cannot account for anything but higher and lower and laterally in terms of the distance from the central axis of those Places considered to be 'civilized.' If you look at the early Sumerian inlaid processional banner with narrative stories depicted on both sides, the so-called *Royal Standard*.' Horizontal registers separate three horizontal scenes on each side. This beautiful work of art was found in the Royal cemetery at Ur, the Sumerian capitol (Place). It appears at a place considered one of the earliest city states in human history, originating about 3800 BCE. The language spoken there was very different from all of the succeeding people who ruled Mesopotamia. On both sides of this banner is a hierarchical distribution of scenes. The two sides complement each other, one depicting 'War' the other 'Peace.'

http://www.britishmuseum.org/research/collection_online/collection_object_details/collection_image_gallery.aspx?assetId=12550001&objectId=368264&partId=1#more-views

"It is called the "Standard of Ur" because it was once thought to be a two-sided banner. However, the end panels holding mythical beasts are pyramidal suggesting the object was the sound box of a harp or some kind of musical instrument.

"The War side shows a battle in the lowest register with charioteers conquering an enemy. The next scene shows the generals on one side leading the prisoners of war in a parade of captives where at the top they meet the ruler who holds a staff bound with yarn to receive them. In this centered composition, the three registers of the story demonstrate a hierarchy of less to most important as one reads the panel historically from bottom to top."

X, isn't that just a way of depicting space when a Renaissance view of three-dimensional space just wasn't possible at that time?

"Possibly, but that does not detract from the formula of holiest at the top, least holy at the bottom, or closest to the would-be viewer.

"On the Peace side, the upper most register of the three is occupied by the heads of the society, the upper class if you will. The second register down represents a middle class, on one side the captains and warriors who have defeated the enemy, then laborers, farmers, and stockmen who bring prosperity to the king. He and his men, and implicitly to the community shown in the scene above, enjoy the victory.

http://www.britishmuseum.org/research/collec-
tion_online/collection_object_details/collection_im-
age_gallery.aspx?assetId=12550001&objectId=368264&par-
tId=1#more-views

"In the lowest, third register are lower class people laboring bringing their animals and heavy crops guided by a central "manager" whereas above in the middle register a larger-sized group of people appears delivering festooned cattle and sheep, clearly a 'middle class,' also guided by one of the king's viziers. At the top, the king and his court enjoy the fruits of their subjects' labor, drinking, feasting, honoring the larger figure of the King as smaller sized people play a harp the other clasps his/her hands.

"This remarkable work of art made up of a mosaic of colored stone impressed into bitumen as glue impressed over wooden panels. Its form is characteristic of all early civilized narrative art. Narrative is always subordinate to social stratification but the story itself justifies the hierarchy. While Vertical culture has three-dimensionality, in fact, it is always conceptually two-dimensional whether you are looking at more abstract forms found in ancient Egyptian art or more humanistic forms and narratives in Greek art."

I don't know, X. It doesn't seem much like ancient Greek or Egyptian art.

"In Egyptian tombs and Greek pottery the top-to-bottom sequence of scenes is arranged hierarchically from the most holy, abstract, and powerful to the less powerful, more human, and even descriptive narrative to animals and plants or abstract design at the base. In all of these cases the registers (two-dimensional bands separating narrative pictorial space) have this Vertical hierarchy as an imperative to demonstrate a Hierarchical Order from the lowest and least, to the upper and more valued strata in the society. It defines who fits where in that hierarchy including the natural world. That separation of man from nature is usually designated to

41

the lowest registers, defining superior man as superior to nature."

> Nature seems to become totally symbolic if
> represented at all, but that doesn't apply now.
> Modern art since the Renaissance doesn't seg-
> ment scenes like that, does it?

"We will get to that. In the meantime, do not be deceive
that hierarchical art does not continue into your time. Just
think, TED001, of what this hierarchical separation means in
terms of slavery, crushing of the physical autonomy, creative
spirit, destroying identity, destroying the natural world, in-
clusiveness, and inventiveness within the narrowest parame-
ters. Free thought is deliberately suppressed. Bullying and
enslavement are direct products of Vertical Society. Because
Vertical Societies can become so complex in their organization and overlapping of powers, a widespread confusion occurs among even the greatest minds operating in this hierarchical environment. Vertical thinking rarely permits creative
minds unless designated to a labeled specialization, which
necessarily reinforces Vertical power and control."

> I have to say, X, it does seem like a natural pro-
> cess instead of creating a hierarchical caste
> system. Animals define their territories by
> brute strength, males over weaker adversaries,
> or animals that mark their territories with
> their urine. It probably seems like a natural
> distribution of power and authority. Smart
> people need to be in charge because they know
> or can figure out what to do when 'change' or
> a threat arrives, where others cannot act deci-
> sively.

"TED001, please stop. I am amazed you repeat these fallacious, delusional concepts. They are a direct product of Vertical Hierarchical Society unconsciously embedded in you.
Unfortunately, you present them as if they are 'natural,' a
common Vertical argument for all kinds of injustices waged

against any arbitrary target whenever it suits Vertical authorities and expressions of power.

> Yeah. O.K. Whenever you call me 'TED001,' I
> know you are not happy with me. Sorry, maybe
> that's the wrong word for an EBE.

"Staying on point. Discrimination against women, for example, is not only a cowardly, bullying act, but a form of enslavement. Too many Terran men are of such weak character that they sell their daughters to the highest bidder, or even murder them without regard to her humanity or awareness that the human chromosomes are shared equally by offspring from mother and father.

"In rigid, sharply Vertical Societies women are also dressed in costumes that shell their bodies in another prison of cloth, sometimes dressing in forms reaching generations back in time. For these acutely tribalistic Vertical Societies, acknowledgement of images, ideas, and systems outside their own seem to pose the greatest threat to their unsubstantiated customs and mythologies. These hardened hierarchies, especially religious ones, also suffer the most as they transfer out of the Vertical Society into a pluralistic and Holographic ones. In this transition, political posturing and reactionary blood-letting reaches obscene levels.

"Those in the upper strata of Vertical, especially extremely despotic cultures, usually have a bodyguard of would-be ascendants on the Vertical elevator, often in a presumptive divinely disposed 'Right to Rule.'

"It takes many forms of unwarranted and unjustified privilege, as in lineages of inherited wealth, position, authority, resulting in idiot kings, megalomanic generals, the courtiers and political attachés and the fanatically religious to become fatuous, debased, pompous displays flouting their privileges, having nothing more to contribute than their fatuous ostensibility and wonton inhumanity."

> So, the thing that you said was worse than the
> plague is nothing other than Vertical Society
> itself?

"Perhaps I should have said insidious rather than plague. The Plague is too kind. The plague, unlike Vertical Society, spares many."

AUTHORITARIAN VERTICAL SOCIETIES

> I think most of us humans are really sick of political posturing, pomp, and tomfoolery, the seeming *'Ships of Fools,' 'Confederacies of Dunces'* in power.

"TED it's much more sinister and debilitating than you imagine. For all the words spoken or written, human beings in hierarchical strategies can only think of alternative methods for enslaving themselves. You do this in a thousand different ways to use a loose expression. You are all prisoners, slaves of your failure to mature in a timely manner. To anyone outside your little blue marble planet, it is disturbing that your mental and social development has gone only as far as it has."

> Look, many of us have developed to the point that some of us realize you were here possibly for a long time. We successfully communicated with your species when it made a crop circle at Chilbolton, England, in response to Karl Sagan's message sent into deep space twenty years earlier.

"Congratulations! So, you made a crack in the egg. Again, I must remind you that your answers or should I say 'reactions' to my remarks, miss the mark. Unfortunately, they represent only a superficial comprehension of my statement. You answer cites a technological feat as if that is the only measure of man. If we did not have other examples of this kind of mis-measure in other worlds we would not believe you could escape the trap you have set for yourselves."

> What do you mean, 'trap?'

"You are trapped in your servility, your inherent slavehood to gravity based verticality."

> What do you mean slavehood? I'm a free man as are millions of others.

"Your slavehood is owed to all that you think to be valuable--religion, technology, culture, political systems, economic systems, philosophies, all of which are based on your identity with Place."

Wow, what's left? You are saying that we humans are slaves to everything, everything we create for our survival, everything we hold dear?

"Now you are getting closer. Precisely, it is your focus on survival, or to put in another way your focus on death and more accurately on extinction that enslaves you, constraining you to the most primitive and barbaric conditions in virtually every Terran community."

But of course! If we did not have religion, politics, culture, political and economic systems, and technology, we would not survive and mankind would rather quickly become extinct. So, I ask, is your civilization so advanced technologically that you do not need or have any of these kinds of institutions? I mean, how did you, get here, by a happy thought? Besides Place is not as important as it once was. Why do you put so much importance on it?

"Once again, your slavery is built into your language. Your language construct suggests that what enables inter-galactic life to exist is strictly a technological feat. You seem convinced that technology and the science that supports it is a measure of your survivability. So, let me ask you this: Among all the earth's great philosophers, religious, writers, artists, philosophers, leaders in your advanced educational systems, how many see technology as the only means for improving the success of your species to survive the death, the extinction that you so greatly fear?"

I can't think of any, at least not right now.

"Fearing extinction you practice extinction. Look at how millions who die from religious, economic, ideological, and political conflicts in what you call war. After 'death' and 'extinction,' 'war' is one of your favorite words and activities. If you don't change your language, death and extinction will overrun your specie. Your slavery is built into your Vertical language and your fear of death and extinction. Why, TED, is it so difficult to accept it as the truly natural process that it is?"

> I'm not sure where you are going with this X. I can tell you I don't think of death, my own or anyone else's very often, and while I am a little worried about nuclear and biological weapons, global warming and pandemics every now and then, I rarely think of human extinction. I don't buy into the Muslim 'hellfire' or the Christian 'apocalypse'.

"If you don't, most of your fellow Americans do. Their T-shirts are covered with death's heads, or crosses with death heads. The same icon appears in you videos and films, on railroad cars, trailer hitches, wall paintings. Your religions are hopelessly preoccupied with apocalypse and make most of their money from people terrified that their soul will be either cast into an eternal hell or that it will become annihilated altogether. Individual passing of your life form is transferred by religion at the cessation of your bodily functions is a mythical next life. Your egos, being what they are, your chief deities become so angry with their own creation of the human specie they choose to suicidally end the whole universe, religiously speaking. Fortunately for the rest of us, you religions of death and the antidote 'resurrection' are limited to planet earth."

> Religions in general seem to have a lot of inconsistencies, I guess. No matter how much good work might be done in the name of this or that religion, prophet or deity, religions do seem to separate and fragment. It does bother me that each religious sect claims to have been given the truth, the unique and one-and-only truth.
> Its true, if someone does not believe a group belief or view it in the same way, dissenters,

47

critical thinkers are considered less than human are considered anathema, blasphemous, and unworthy of existence.

Islam, for example, claims 'Infidels' must be killed. Christianity claims that if unbelievers are not punished in this lifetime, they will be in the next with the expectation of suffering the worst possible tortures and eternal fire. I admit, sectarian religions are a significant problem every politician and so-called leader indulges in, if for no other reason, for the blessings and support of the ignorant and ignoble masses and true believers.

"To continue. Religions are products of Vertical Societies with their axes centered at sacred sites. Those locations are always politico-religious in origin and iconological focal points. Place becomes sacrosanct if not magically sacred. It doesn't matter if it is Borobudur, Jerusalem, Calcutta, Chartres, or Mecca, these sacred sites are designated for the believers to prove to fantasy divine entities that they are true believers, especially if they make an effort to visit these sites.

"Everything about Place lies with Magical Thinking based on authority? Authority is sometimes attached to an object or book, most originally hand copied in a form of writing the masses could in no way read or understand at the time those 'sacred' books were written and hidden in libraries admissible to only the most trusted and initiated believers. Not knowing how to read or write in their own native speech, to say nothing of the arcane and secretive languages of the priesthood, which compiles and rewrites it, these texts are regarded as magical. These words were for over a thousand years in Western Europe and elsewhere professed to be and were in fact considered divinely transmitted and entirely magical.

"For example, Northumbrian scribes in tiny, 8th century (CE) monasteries knew neither Latin nor the source of symbols, they were required to place in these texts. Their work became acts of pious and magical devotion. A sacred book acquires sacred authority because it is supposed to contain divine messages. It has beautiful hand scripts or sacred images to enhance this perception. Even the scribe-illuminators may not have understood their meaning, but with meticulous care and the finest craftsmanship considered in representations of sacred and symbolic, endowed these books with magical power.

"Objectness in the form of books, scripts, images of symbols, images of putative divine beings gives tangible reality to the naïve and gullible who usually know nothing about anything in their entire world."

X, let's be real. We have to accept authority somewhere in our lives, otherwise there would be chaos. If I should blow through a red light at an intersection and hit another vehicle, I could accidentally kill or maim one or more people including myself.

"So you seem to suggest that if there was not a law about running a red light, you would have no authority. Your real explanation of authority is that you have a natural, inbuilt authority called self-preservation that is really at issue in the example you give. Laws based on practical knowledge and experience constitute an authority that is tangible and used as a means of controlling fateful events such as the one you describe. It is a position based on Evidence, evidence that leads to rational objectives, formulas and laws.

"Religious, mystic or prophetic authority has no practicality or foundation at all. These "authorities" serve only those on the supreme levels of hierarchy and have nothing to do with a general benefit to the human community. It is simply a form of brute force, bullying on a colossal scale, usually enforced by psychological terror and physical or economic catastrophe rather than by practical rules designed to protect everyone for the greatest good."

You are saying all religions are based on brute authority.

"No. Not at all! I am saying they are all based on Magical Thinking rather than practical, rational, or logical thinking. Stained glass windows, beautiful prayers, poetry, beautiful architecture, mosaics, scripts, music, and sculptures disguise the fact that it facilitates control in a Vertical state. Why do you think the formulators of the U.S. Constitution separated church from state? They belonged to what is called the 'Age of Reason.'"

> X, when someone claims they have divine authority documented in a book, like the Bible, Torah, or Koran, they have legal authority to make the claims that they do, either because of their theological knowledge or because of divine inspiration.

"Yes, exactly, that is the standard argument along with the necessity that one must 'believe' or 'have faith' or the promises of the books will not be fulfilled and all human life will be consumed and condemned. Unfortunately, without verifiable authority, that authority is nothing more than a delusion created by Magical Thinking, which in its religious formulations constitute "dogma." Inherent to Magical Thinking regarding belief and faith, there is an implicit notion that if everyone does not think the same way, or wear the same clothes as other members of their sex and sect, cover their head or face because they are a woman, or for men to have a full beard or must be clean shaven, or wear a special headdress, their religion and all that they know will collapse. I am suggesting, indeed it should, as it is nothing but theater manifesting expressions of hierarchy."

> Those are cultural things, right?

"Tribal identifiers, yes. You humans are very object-oriented and confuse object with the thing it supposedly represents. This is precisely what Hindi's, Moses, and Mohammed sought to deliver their people from by disposing of images, be they cows, snakes, or saintly humanoids. However, those images, those other '*gods before you*,' can be given dress, costume, sexual obsession, engage in drug and alcohol abuse, recite stock prayers, and accumulate vast material possessions and wealth at the expense of all others on the planet. All images, sacred or not, are '*objects of worship*' meant to express 'power over,' and detract from the real message being delivered.

"Each religion, as a racial, linguistic and tribal identity, compounds this problem by separating itself on a physical as well as an ideological level from the rest of humanity. That separation contributes to the dissention and turmoil of your world. Christians wear crosses, Jews 'stars of David' and yam akas, beanies or funny hats to set themselves apart from the rest of humanity as if having been chosen by a supreme deity to be part of a particular racial (tribal) group or even a more righteous, holier subset of a larger group of believers among the majestic and magical authority images.

"It is a clear corruption of documentable history and unsubstantiated by evidence. Another example: Israel is first mentioned in chronicles of the Egyptian king Thutmoses III's war against the towns of the Levant, consummating in the defeat of the town of Megiddo. Thutmoses settled for a while on a hill of which later became Jerusalem, built a palace that today Jews prefer to believe was the foundation of Solomon's temple, which it may well have been centuries later. After the conquest of Megiddo, Thutmoses III could claim on carvings in the temple at Karnak that he had conquered territory up to the Euphrates River. Early Biblical authors identify Thutmoses III with David even create two Davids who had to have lived at two different times to account for the discrepancy with historical fact. Modern Jews claim that this first 'David' you should know is Thutmoses III conquered all of the territory to the Tigris River. Jews pray at the palace foundations of Thutmoses III, thinking they belonged to David (both pseudo-Davids) and Solomon."

You know, I did see a ground plan of Solomon's temple and it was astonishingly similar to the plans of the temple at Karnak Egypt.

"If we look at the iconographies of the fifth century CE in the great church of Santa Maria Maggiore, Rome, we find mosaics celebrating the separation of believers from non-believers, '*Jesus separating the sheep* (Christians) *from the goats* (non-Christians), or the mosaic of *The Separation of Lot* (the sinful) *and Abraham* (Christian forbearers). These are poisonous acts of deliberate distortions of history perpetuated by a combined alliance between racial superiority and a fanticized authority based on delusions collectively and interchangeably called 'religion' and 'culture.' They were intentionally racist. Ultimately, these kinds of hierarchical thoughts and separating concepts threaten the survival of the human specie.

"The more you make this separation from each other the more you condemn your future."

> Yes, I see how an unconscious separation of everybody from each other based on assumptions of Vertical Hierarchy can be so damning to the lesser groups who become victims. It's really sad.

"Until every member of this planet realizes they must now see each other as related and are part of an organic Holographic whole of nature and man in a unified and integrated cosmos, your world is unsafe. Thanks to the 'Human Genome Project,' all of you are brothers and sisters traceable to central Africa. You are all Africans, like it or not, no matter what the color of your skin or hair, shape, or facial features. No one is selected out by any God as 'chosen' or superior human beings who have the holier or holiest, most hidden secrets of life. Your family genes do that for you. Culture is just as much a constraint on human liberty and dignity as religion. How you tolerate either of them is hard to understand. Wait 'til you meet some of us."

> I really want to do that, I think, but how does your society handle death? You do die, don't you? Religions help with death here on earth, especially family members to cope with their loss. Do you honor your dead, have funerals? Is there really a heaven?

"Yes. Perhaps we should discuss that tomorrow."

LOG VI

PAIN, SUFFERING, AND DEATH:
RELIGIONS' SOLUTIONS

I understand X that when the first EBE's were
captured by the U.S. military, one of the questions they were asked was *Is there a God.*

"Yes, they asked that, and if we did not know human history we would have been utterly confused. So, you raise the
question because you want the answer yourself, right?"

It is a kind of back-handed way of asking, I
suppose, but Yes.

"In the words of your common street language: 'Oh,
crap!' The major question, here, is less than what or who is
God, Allah, Yahweh, Jehovah, and so on through the panthe-
ons of tens of thousands of human deities, but why do you
think you need to know?"

It's because it is the most important question
we can ask. If there is a God, then it partially
answers who we are, where we come from and
where we are going, questions even a simple
man like the painter Paul Gauguin asks in a
work of art by that title: *Who Are We, Where
do We Come From, and Where are We Going?*
What is human purpose?

"TED, in your own simplistic way, you partially answered the question, but got confused by the necessity of a
having a supreme being on the Vertical hierarchy in your
mind. I hope that you understand by now that just about everyone capable of visiting this little blue marble from another
star system or galaxy knows they are already 'supreme beings,' compared to any TED."

X, why do you have to put us down? You mean
in terms of intelligence or our evolutionary
point in history?

"There, now you have it. You instantly become defensive
of that part of yourself you call the Self. It is from that concept
of Self your necessity arises for a supreme creator or being
springs. It is a need for a Vertical being that transcends all

other Vertical supremacies, mostly because you inherently know those at the top of your vertical hierarchies are flawed human beings, with less sapiens than their subjects.

"Having failed on all accounts to understand the universe and how it got to be, you project onto the cosmos a cosmology of the Self. You say to yourselves: '*I am an intelligent species, smart enough to know that there are reasons for the way things are and forces link together and unlink, come into conscious existence then fade or die.*' Is that a fair statement? Based on your sense of self, you assume if there is logic to the universe, there must be an all-powerful intelligence that planned it all. You say to yourself, something just a whole lot smarter than me has created the universe and it must be an divine entity, strictly male, of course, who fathers everything into existence. Is that not what you believe? "

I think so. Is that an ontological, teleological,
theological, or cosmological statement?

"TED, please stop trying to put labels on everything. Yes, I understand labels help control your concept of virtually everything, but labels do not answer the question of the existence of God, or human purpose, least of all because you have the audacity to give this concept a single name, like the word "God." You are really asking the question of existence about existence. Tibetan monks do better by claiming there are an infinite number of names of God. Labeling is big TED business. Money is made off of symbolic labels. More people and more thought go into the design and information on a can of soup for your supermarkets than a thousand minds in a thousand monasteries and theological schools about the labels of god and godly and what they and it tell us."

O.K., Go on. I'm with you now.

"In a previous discussion we already observed how the human being develops a sense of self, how that self can either be a radiant joy to and for the world or become something profoundly damaged and damaging. What I want to propose to you now is that your necessity for seeking a superior Supreme Being, both on earth and off, has led to all kinds of earthly cults, sects, religions, all of which have only one thing in common, their desire to destroy anyone or any group that is 'different'."

Can't imagine what that would be if it isn't the existence of God.

"Precisely. It's a strictly human flaw, but adhered to above all others."

O.K., O.K. Please get to the point.

"Every human group thinks they have the ineffable answer to the questions of deity, supernatural powers, and human purpose, which no other group has. All religions are by their nature mutually exclusive on the simple premise their ancestors or predecessors got the correct version, or the only version, making them the "chosen ones," and everyone else is mistaken or unloved by God. In good times that mistaken assumption will allow people to co-habit the earth, but in all cases there is a tension that never dissipates between one answer to the questions of *Who are we, Where do we come from. Where are We Going.*

"In times of stress between groups, humans practice all the vileness their own religious precepts forbid. To kill, maim, commit genocide, is one of the favorite human pastimes, especially if the sect or religion intentionally or inadvertently damages or destroys the healthy development of the Self. It varies, but all Vertical Societies and their subsets incapacitate the self even using the silly (syllogistic) argument *'You're being selfish if you talk about the importance of the self.'*"

I have to admit our religions, especially the 'Great Religions,' commit the most horrific crimes in the name of their gods, deities, and sometimes totally misguided values based on nothing other than it is 'traditional,' or what is written, in a 'sacred,' that is, magical book.

"Exactly, what is traditional, what is one cultural paradigm as opposed to another, is the residue of a tribalistic or ancestral view of the universe designed to protect the damaged Self. The Biblical story of Creation of Adam and Eve is in itself, damaging to the human Self. When you look at the universe from a cosmic view as opposed to the tribalistic one, the religio-cultural ones no longer have any validity.

"'Culture' operates compatibly and inseparably with religion. Both are inhibiting psychological and social growth. When you worry about death and extinction, it is really about the dissolution of Self and not just the local 'chosen' or 'saved' Order of Things."

Now, I am getting confused. You are implying so many things that I think I would have to have an encyclopedic mind to cope with them.

"Well that might help you a bit, although I doubt it. May I continue?"

Hmp.

"TED, just a reminder, you and I are having this conversation as an explanation as to why the cosmic community cannot yet accept human society into the galactic or inter-galactic universe. You think that because your science has brought you into the microcosm of biology, nuclear energy, electric power, and the macrocosm of the universe that you have evolved as your concept of what an all-powerful, omnipotent, and omniscient god intended. For us, you have simply become extremely arrogant and dangerous, both to yourselves and to us. We have learned lessons from similar cultures in which we mistakenly elected not to intervene."

What do you mean 'intervene?' Damn it! That's what we are afraid of, extraterrestrials attacking us, destroying human existence with super weapons, or vaporizing our oceans, or killing us with pandemics or nerve agents or just eating us.

I would really like to have an answer, and that is the main reason for my fear about communicating with you. If you are so smart, there are no ways we can compete with an intelligence that can think more deeply and quickly than our greatest computers. This is the really important question. How do you plan to intervene with us?"

"*Calmé, Calmé!* Because of your lack of Self, you lack integrity. Your thoughtless compulsions compel you to find solutions, in violence you believe any other intelligent life in the universe will act in the same way as you. Your perception of everything outside of the earth is seen through the stained glass of your sociopathy, tribalism, and Vertical thinking.

"Galactically, we have our own histories of catastrophes as do others. Everything you describe as a threat posed by extraterrestrial contact is actually your own, first imagined, then codified in books and computers, of well-planned and developed systems for total annihilation of the human race, when you are the greatest danger to yourselves by your Magical Thinking supporting the artificial structure of Vertical hierarchy."

What do you mean?

"You know, right now that you could destroy all life on earth with your current nuclear weapons standing at trigger-readiness; that every village and city on the planet with a population of 1,400 people or more has been systematically targeted with nuclear weapons probably no smaller than a megaton?"

Yes and no. I didn't know that so many places had been targeted. Only 1,400 people? How stupid. What for?

"To say nothing of global warming, starvation even in the most wealthy of countries is already occurring including your own."

Yes, I know that. But why are military planners wanting to destroy every town and village on the planet?

"Exactly. Good question. Doomsday planning with nuclear and other weapons of mass destruction are part of the infamous: '*I'd rather be dead than red*' vertical mentality. People who make those kinds of statements have no knowledge of history, of how transient culture is, or how inhumane and absolutist their suicidal Magico-Vertical thinking is. You have no idea of how much and how great human suffering and unnecessary death occurs and exists throughout your planet. It is a constant and horrific threat. Between

57

political and economic threats and ideological religious threats, the latter will most likely bring an end to the human race."

> Probably not. Yes, there are radical Islamic
> threats but they don't have nuclear bombs or
> the ability to send them here.

"You mean not yet. No, you have no idea what to do about the perfidy of Vertical Thinking, human suffering and mass death, either. Neither does anyone else on your beautiful blue planet. So, now, would you like to see an intervention? Or shall we move on leaving you with your fatal flaws and inevitable suicidal assumptions?"

> I guess people pray for peace and well-being
> for themselves and everyone every day. For
> most people it is probably because they think
> they believe truths no one else knows or ac-
> cepts that when the end of life comes as we
> know it, they, unlike others, will be chosen by
> a Gracious God. Christians talk about the 'End
> Times' and Islamists about the 'Hell Fire,' as
> mentioned before."

"You were worried about an extraterrestrial threat of intervention a moment ago, right? You are so utterly benign about what you humans are doing and planning to do to yourselves and to each other, and unknowingly to your entire solar system! Now, tell me the kind of intervention you think any civilization which has successfully passed the stage you humans are presently encountering, one would think about your global social order based on ancient fantasies and formulas based on Vertical Places and Vertical hierarchies of authority."

> I think we might want to blow it up wondering
> how we could possibly live in a totally inte-
> grated and holistic world without religion and
> social customs, however tribal.

"Oh, my aunt's toenail! Here is the 'Death of the World Self' again. I cannot believe you! Instantly, your solution is apocalypse. 'Blow it up!' This world into which you find yourself is not yours. It does not belong exclusively to you, you arrogant humans! You may have power over terrestrial plants and animals, but that works both ways. In your hands it ultimately means, by your instantaneous answers and insouciance, utter destruction of all life is your only choice; so, why not make a profit and whore the world out into a materialistic nightmare?"

I am smarter than you think. You just swore
but did not use God's name in vain. So, I can
conclude there is no God to swear about when
you're angry!

"There is no necessity for a super-divine or mythological beings in this or any other solar system, galaxy, or universe. Neither religion nor deities are necessary for morality, nor are they necessary to explain life here or anywhere else except to the most simple minded. Deities cannot save you from death, pain, or suffering, poor health, by giving miracle healings or good crops. Prayers are merely another delusion you like to indulge in as if some deity would listen to you more preferably more than someone else. We all understand how we want to do something when tragedy strikes, but prayers? If you can enter a telepathic mode such a prayer might very well work, otherwise it is largely an act of empty piety, at best, prayer is a legitimate form of meditation and relaxation."

Most people do not seem afraid of death, so,
why do you think we are controlled by it?

"Dear TED. Another thing we EBE's have learned is to have great patience with people of shorter histories. Let's let you chew on these things for a while; then, we will get back with each other when you are ready.

"I have presented what you would regard as a megahistorical view of intelligent life in your solar system. I want to share that with you accenting your current dilemma. We and others have a long history with intelligent life here in your place in the midst of the ocean of stars and planets in our galaxy.

"You have never been alone. Let's talk about human life and death and how you are star people, ineffable beings just like us, all made of stardust and belong to the firmament you so desperately in your fears want to label and fear."

Uh, yes, I want to hear that. X? X? Oh, you've left haven't you? I hope he comes back.

LOG VII

CULTS OF LIFE AND DEATH, YIN AND YANG

"Ah, you are just beginning to wake up."

I am awake or are you speaking metaphorically?

"Make your choice. TED. For me you humans are always asleep. In this morning hour of emerging wakefulness, I need to discuss with you your most destructive delusional object of thinking and preoccupation."

I know, human life and death in the artifices of
Vertical Society.

"It amazes us that you humans have devolved into a culture of death. While death is part of nature, you humans are obsessed with it. With what your science already knows, it is incomprehensible that your every act seems to be about death. Your religions are all about death and what is supposed to happen after your organism ceases to symbiotically function. You build and use armies of death and commit indiscriminate mass murder. In your country you are obsessed with guns from the smallest to military size weapons that no other country in your world allows its people to own or carry. Your people act as if the Second Amendment to your Constitution is sacred, a basic, inviolable human right. You wear military camophlage costumes as civilian wear and put death's heads everywhere, forgetting the U.S. Constitution is a creation and adaptable.

"As I already mentioned, we see death's heads on tee-shirts, jackets, tattoos, even on trailer hitches with red lights for Devil eyes. How hideous and laughable you make human death. How barbaric the rationales made to justify these things.

"This preoccupation you have is sociopathy, just as religion itself is a form of sociopathy mistakenly thought to be protective, salvific, and somehow moral. There is no reality here, only delusion for which most peoples of this and other galaxies consider odious and mindless. What a bunch of

61

knuckle heads...one of my favorite words I have adopted from you."

> You must well know, X, that when that right to bear arms was written into the U.S. Constitution in the 1700's there was both a great fear of an imperial government represented by England and most other imperialized European countries at that time. Their inclusion of that amendment was based on the necessity of a citizen army that should be available at a moment's notice, one group called 'Minute Men' for that reason. The other factor was that the level of technology of hand-held weapons as existed at that time has changed radically since then.

"Yes, and instead of addressing that fact in a non-delusional way, the claim is made that you have the right to overthrow an unjust, corrupt, and oppressive government, right?"

"That argument is sometimes made in Texas, but rabidly in Montana, Nebraska, and Idaho, the latter a home of the Neo-Nazis who wish to overthrow the government. Thomas Jefferson wrote that people should be able to rise up against an oppressive government in his Declaration of Independence, but it is not part of the American Constitution and no citizens with guns today could overthrow a military army with trained military of which you now have many in every town to meet any such rebellion."

To be sure!

"Yet, you have a government which is all of those oppressive and corrupt things at this very moment and what are the results when individuals or groups would attempt to overthrow a government with sophisticated weapons?"

Our government isn't that bad.

"No, of course not! Everyone would be in the streets with their guns, wouldn't they? It is really not that bad. The people who commit revolution against the government are either killed or jailed, especially if they should peacefully protest and run the risk of being beaten, tortured or labeled and ostracized for life as being a threat to the present Order, in your case, the Constitution and the State. The more despotic the state, the more powers will become abusive toward the average citizen."

I don't think you are giving the full picture. Most of the people who do these things are suicidal or mentally disturbed, or chronically unemployed.

"It would seem that way, if we had to listen to your reinterpretations of the 'news,' but I don't believe so. What you say in the narrower context is true. Disturbed people do rebel. Your 'Founding Fathers' stood against the most powerful army in the world at that time and challenged the most sacrosanct idea, the ideal of the imperial state, run, as always, by absolute authority sanctioned by the Church of England in that case and by churches all over Europe at that time. Your forefathers were quite disturbed by the outrageous behavior of those imperial hierarchies and they saw the Colonists as outrageous barbarians.

"It is not only absolute (i.e. 'divinely appointed') authority that the attribution was made at the time. Do not think for a minute TED001 that anyone in positions of absolute authority does not maintain the delusion of divine dispensation for themselves as the most beloved and deserving in the eyes and mind of their hierarchic and homocentric deities."

We Americans had a lot of space at the time in those days, X. People like to be left alone to their creations, their families, their pleasures, their possessions.

"Where are you going with this argument?"

Remember Jefferson's claim to our right to *'life, liberty, and the pursuit of happiness?'* Divine authority was hardly apparent to the framers of the Constitution, whether in the country, village, or emerging cities. They had seen where it had taken man for millennia. We did however cover our money with symbols of divine dispensation, when it seemed we had

succeeded in defeating the English monarchy,
the influence of the Scottish Masons.

"When British rule seemed oppressive or in most instances irrelevant to their lives, imperial taxes, and trade barriers were worth objecting to and ultimate fighting against, but not by all, especially those living in cities. Not only that, in the 18th and early 19th centuries as the colonies were finding a unity of purpose, many read books, books written about the Greek democracy of ancient Athens and the Roman Republic. They read the great British intellectuals Locke and Hume about what was the purpose of government was and which concept, imperium or democracy, would benefit human life the most.

"Even though most were rural farmers, early American citizens were not ignorant like many today. Even those educated in your schools and colleges today cannot differentiate the many institutions, such as formal religions, between liberty and domination. They watch TV or hand-held back-lit devices instead, most of the time fingering a profusion of nonsense. Thomas Jefferson is said to have read as many as a 1,000 books in a solar year by sunlight and candle.

Nobody reads a 1,000 books today nor would
they want to. Americans don't even read news
papers lately.

"Yes, to continue. When the Frenchman Alexis de Tocqueville came to America in the early nineteenth century to find out why democracy seemed to be working in your country and not in his native France, the thing that surprised him most was that Americans were informed. They were knowledgeable about philosophy and politics, imperialism versus democracy, and man's capacity to think rationally. In ways difficult for your fellows to understand today, De Tocqueville was astonished.

"He was even more impressed when he went into the countryside where people lived in small cabins. He found them informed as well as those in cities. He wrote a big book called *Democracy in America*. You ought to read it TED. You will see how far astray your people have come."

I agree, all of those men who signed the American Constitution were rebels, risking their
lives opposing the great top-down monarchy
of Britain. Their words and actions were remarkable in the face of oppression and the
daily difficulties of everyday life as it was.
Americans wanted to protect an idea that
would work better than monarchy and imperial dynasties did elsewhere. Are you the least
aware of that history, X?

"Yes, indeed, I am. Remember, as one who was chosen
and chose to communicate with this fitful and slowly matur-
ing human race. You earliest citizens were rebelling against
Vertical Society. If you knew my age and our methods of in-
ductive learning, you would understand that I know your literature, your many quests deeply and well. So the question
now is how did you and the rest of the people of this blue orb
become so preoccupied with death and mass destruction?"

Like you said, it's what religious prophesies
foretell. Self-defense, too, I suppose. It seems
that we reached a point in our technology
where it is too dangerous to use massive weapons of destruction, or try to construct peaceful
islands somewhere out in space.

"Yes, that is exactly what the galactic community among
you is most concerned about. You cannot escape what you do
not understand or acknowledge. You take your ignorance, delusions, and troubles with you wherever you go. So, there is
no room for you presently except on a minor level within your
own solar system.

"Deep space is already taken. We are not about to let you
or any formative, undeveloped race entry into the deeper universe without a clear understanding of the lessons learn-ed in
the billions of years of ubiquitous life in this and every galaxy.
But let's not abandon our objective here. Why do you think
you have a preoccupation with death?"

Obviously, we all know we are going to die someday.
Vita brevis est, as they say! Now that you have me
thinking about it, maybe I think about it a lot. Yes, we

dress in death images, because we are trying to embrace our personal and global death using these images. Maybe we want to have control over our personal and collective death by making death and extinction possible to contemplate.

"You are getting a little closer to a truth. Look at Christians in most of the world who adorn their churches and bedroom walls with images of a man crucified, or an image of the cross. It is a vehicle for identifying with suffering and death. You would never know from these paintings and sculptures their religion was fundamentally about rebirth. In your preoccupation with death you miss the major objective and promise of the Christian message. With such flipping discourse, you wonder why the intergalactic community does not want to give you full access? Religious theologies represent more involved theological premises than your wish for control over one's own and a collective death."

How do you mean, X?

"Apart from intrinsic human behaviors common to both men and women, there are differences between your sexes accounting for some of the perpetual saber rattling. You have a problem with your propagation of the species; namely, that dual entities must copulate in order to perpetuate. In that context you have the notion that males dominate females and that is the natural order of things."

Actually, we like that, most of the time.

"Understandable, and nature throughout the universe is magnificently abundant and found everywhere, regardless of how it is propagated and perpetuated, sometimes assigning male domination in others female. However, remember Karl Sagan's digital message sent into space describing human life on this planet. His message identified a difference."

Yes, of course. We talked about that.

"So, he sent the information describing that you are carbon-based beings with two strands of DNA and along with much other information, including two anthropomorphic sketches of a man and a woman."

Yes, quite amazing, ingenious, I think. Bril-
liant man, especially having sent that image in
1974 via the Arecibo giant radio telescope.

"Well, he helped Frank Drake make the message, but what I am trying to get to is the fact that 22 years later, across space and time, his message was answered in an English field of grain next to and axially oriented toward England's largest radio telescope as a "fractal crop glyph" at Chilbolton, Hampshire, England. "

Yes, that is intentional and amazing along with
a profile view of an EBE's head. For me that
was the most conclusive evidence that humans
were not alone in the universe...God's preferred. Bye the way, are those your features
too?

"No. We'll discuss that later. Sagan also sent an engraved bronze plaque attached to Apollo 10 which also gave more explicit information about human male and female anatomies and Psi proportions you mentioned earlier. On the same plaque are representations of the sun and all of the planets of your solar system, thinking that the odds of another civilization in solar or galactic space might find this plaque on such a tiny piece of space junk in the vastness of the home galaxy and wider universe.

"Quite an expectation, you think? It's something like throwing a bottle into the ocean with a note inside. What do you think happened with Apollo 10 and its plaque?"

I imagine it's still flying through space, unknown to any intelligent being and will probably be unknown until it collides with an object
in space or gets drawn into the interior or orbit
of another sun.

"Such optimists, you humans! To your surprise, no doubt, we and others knew about the plaque and the orbit long before it left the gravity of the earth."

Uhh! You mean you are able to see what's going on here on earth from vast distances.

"Technically, we can do that, but TED001, understand we are here with you, now. We and others of the galactic community have been here for thousands of millennia. We are in a sense your guardians and gardeners. Over thousands of years, our actions, occasional interventions, and images have become part of your images, symbols, and iconographies. We'll discuss that later. In the meantime, let's return to the topic at hand."

What's that? I've lost track. I'm feeling woozy.

"O.K., we were discussing one of the tragic flaws in human biometry, particularly with the male sex."

What do you mean male biometry?

"I am referring to the concepts of male-female and their biological origins. They are true dichotomies throughout nature and the universe. *Vive la difference*, as the French say, but in your present state of evolution maleness and everything between male and female differences is a great source of confusion, often characterized by violence, and commonplace inequities and injustice."

How do you mean, X? Men and women both have   distinctively   different   anatomies, thought processes and social functions.

"Not quite so fast. Your own biological science has shown how genetics plays the apparent determining role, and regardless of the number of people on the planet, nature divides males and females in roughly equal numbers as you know from statistical data on the number of males to females across the entire blue globe. Females have what biologists label double-X chromosomes and men one X and one Y chromosome. Do you see where I am going now?"

Possibly. Are you implying that because the male becomes a male because he has a bit of both the female X and male Y chromosome that the male has an internal genetic link to females?

"Yes and here is the source of several misinterpretations occurring in the concepts of men and women too. Each of the X and Y chromosomes have values, to avoid the links with DNA for the moment, that means the Y chromosome *in utero* can have a very strong X factor that could mean a male may be more effeminate as a male, even though the genitalia are clearly Y, male dominant and the reverse is true for women."

You cannot tell me that there are many variation of maleness and feminity.

"Just look at how some females from a very young age look and act like boys, or that they have physiognomies, voices and tend to take places in life that lean more toward male occupations, social preferences, and costumes of the opposite sex. For some the complexity is greater because there are also hermaphroditic individuals where part of the anatomy is fully female and the genitals are male."

So, what you are saying is that being trans-sexual or "gay" is not a choice, least of all a moral one, but a choice randomly chosen by nature. Just the same, there seems to be more normal people than exceptions.

"Yes, there are to the extent that for whatever reason nature chooses, the human fetus can have a full reversal or partial reversal of sexuality and sexual orientation in its earliest developmental phases. Even in its simplest terms, it is even more complicated than what I describe."

Now you are going to tell me that it is a conscious 'choice' to be 'gay,' homosexual as Christianity and Islam both declare it to be. On the basis of choices people make it's anathema to the moral direction of anyone professing one or the other religion!

"Not quite. Just in the context of religious proscriptions against homosexuality a tragic host of consequences arise among advocates of these or any group or society that speaks of their conceptions. Males and females are finding themselves in artificially, culturally-made, often theological conflict.

"For example, Christians adopt the idea that man (human beings of both sexes) were *Created in the Image of God.* There are no exceptions. Islam has absolute proscriptions of *Hallal* (approved) and *Hallam* (forbidden) regarding sexuality and ancient traditions that reinforce this strict set of its authoritarian judgments. This construct has not always been the case. In ancient Greece and then in ancient Rome homosexuality was regarded with great tolerance, believing that androgyny meant such people born this way were closer to the bi-sexuality or adaptive sexuality of their heaven-dwelling gods."

So, you said there are some other factors in the determination of sexual orientation and even sexual body parts. What would that be?

"Your own scientific discoveries in the second half of the twentieth century discovered another determining factor. When a human fetus is conceived it is neither male nor female, but sometime in the first month after conception, the fetus begins to develop female organs. Then on, or around the 28th or 29th day after conception every mother's brain secretes a flood of male testosterone to her fetus. It is not fully understood why this happens, what triggers it, or how.

"It must have something to do with the presence of that second chromosome. If the fetus is XX, the mother will probably secrete less amounts of testosterone to her fetus whereas the Y chromosome determines that a larger amount of the testosterone would confirm the development of a male fetus. The critical issue is simply that every mother most likely secretes that hormone in different amounts. She has no say in the matter. Nature in all of its randomness is in charge.

"Prayers and wishes notwithstanding, a child's ultimate physiognomy, does not prove sexuality. One team of medical doctors declared that by that logic there are as many variations of sexuality as there are mothers. It is another example where those who bully and persecute observable ambivalences of sexuality in others, have no idea of what modern science has already shown you."

In other words they do not have evidence for discrimination in sexes. I don't see a problem here. If homosexuality is part of a biological process that seems imperfect, then why is maleness and all of its variations a problem? Perhaps you're saying God screwed up again?

"If there was/is one! Let's say it is helpful to avoid theological mumbo jumbo, apologies, and explanations. Androgyny, homosexuality, and all the degrees of femininity and masculinity observable in the human race, have genetic and biological roots that until recently were not understood? How isolated do you have to be to have such ugly prejudices? Have you never walked through a city street, been in gathering of ten or more humans? How can you say that all these variations of sexuality are personality choices? Wake up Terrans. Get out of the wasteland of ignorance and the brain-washed prison cells you call churches, synagogues, and mosques, and just plain non-think."

Isn't that name-calling?

"Prove it! Are you not listening? We can stop here but there are other consequences to consider nature's failure to create absolutes of male and female sexuality. What I would like to suggest to you is that deep in the male brain is an awareness of the male's origin as a female.

"After all, like women, all men have female hormones as well as male. However, it runs even deeper than sharing hormones. Men fear femininity; first their own hidden unconscious origins as females may be troubling to most men. Fearing that they can become a social outcast if they fail to exhibit enough male characteristics weighs heavily on Terran males. Every sports bar is a refuge of the male self, where men of all body types can project on to a video screen the masculine self that really doesn't exist."

Oh, right, X. Now I see where you are going. Oh, yes, a tragic flaw in the psyche and essence of what it means to be male. The consequences of such a driving force completely separate from our conscious sense of who we are as men admittedly can have extreme consequences. From making love, pursuing the opposite sex, wanting sexual unity with them, their very being mirrors of our inner, unconscious self. Men who have broken up with someone they were bonded to sexually and psychically often speak of 'the other half' of

71

their Self as being gone, lost. Or, they might speak of their partner, if even in jest, as '*my better half.*' True?

"An appropriate observation. So, if you can accept the biomorphic creation of the male of the specie, then most of the unpleasant manifestations of maleness become only too obvious. Even though a man may be potent, have many children, he will probably find himself throughout his life making objects, weapons, acting with aggression, aggression against women in general, violence against the female members of his own family and insisting on the rights and rules of manhood, all in defense of an unconscious feminine self. Male children play with weapons and act out mock war almost to obsession.

"Now, with graphic combat video's where young males can partner up electronically with other '*warriors*' in front of their electronic battle displays and play war and killing games, the more gruesome, the more exciting. After all, '*no one is really getting hurt,*' except the people who lose that game. Their maleness, their male self, is effeminized by any kind of defeat.

"In adult life, such male attempts at proving one's maleness can cost trillions in monetary units, millions of lives, and endless suffering. Cast in the guise of personal, national, and other collective interests the consequences of male incompleteness have brought untold misery to the human condition. But you already know that, as instantly as you understand that male aggression is an inherent flaw in the male mind, often evolving into male misogyny."

You don't mean to tell me, X, that the world would be in better order if ruled by women, or that there are no reasons why two sexes are needed to survive, or that there are no serious conflicts that arise for reasons other than male biology. Don't you have males and females, as we find throughout nature, even in plants?

"Yes, of course, but unlike yourselves, male and female are unified in one body. I see a thousand thoughts written all over your face. Suffice it to say, it solves the gender problem, particularly with Terran males and their overcompensations for latent feminine sexuality and self-consciousness. Yes, and to answer the question you are asking yourself, we have solved all of the issues concerning incest, inbreeding and all that goes badly with it. Our mono-sexuality goes well-beyond your current evolution and interest and our heterosexuality thriving, but with none of the 'warfare' between sexes, nor are male hormones a factor in domination, control, violence, and perpetuation of conflict and the cult of death, or the imperium of Vertical Society."

But what is it you are really saying about human male psyches and biology that is so harmful? Is it all about male aggression, need for control, social organization, distribution of labor, wealth, power, authority? Have I left anything out?

For the moment, X, I don't care about discussing extraterrestrial sexuality. What I do know is that between men and women the division of labor is biologically fundamental and our sexual relationships essential to a well-balanced life and mind."

"Good thought! In your present state of evolution, yes. You are not ready to look at it yet, in spite of laws permitting gay and Lesbian marriages to take place. Homosexuality, just like heterosexuality, are functions of nature and depends as we have observed on the mother, a consequence of natural phenomena, not artificially induced, or chosen."

I guess, the definitions of *Yin* and *Yang* are never as absolutely clear as in the Chinese symbol.

LOG VIII
MOTHERHOOD AND THE ORIGINS OF HUMAN SOCIOPATHY

"Terrans live on the edge of extinction because of the social constructs that you think are essential to a 'civil' life, which for the most part work against you. I don't think I need to list them again. As far as your technology is concerned, it is only slightly less developed than your ability to appropriately raise a child. While motherhood is most greatly praised, it is the least skilled on planet earth. For that reason alone, you stand on the precipice and always threatened by people who bring social chaos and potentially global chaos."

X, did your people come with a child-raising manual.

"A rhetorical question, to be sure, if not sarcastic . Like you Terrans, there were no manuals for anything or any one gifted with that knowledge. That does not mean there was not a natural order to pre-human and all life in the universe. It is apparent in the animal world. You have been writing manuals and rewriting them daily and hourly since you became conscious of yourselves. From birth you are naturally protected from complex rational thought so necessary as you pass into adulthood."

X, I think at this point in human development there is general agreement that consciousness in the abstract is very much a part of human nature. For non-literalists, the Garden of Eden story is about the beginning of a consciousness of good and evil. Others observe it is also an example of the capacity to reason, if not always doing it too well.

"A belabored rationale. While I appreciate your insights, let's stay focused on the relationship of human child-rearing and the consequences of its failure for the moment. It is my effort for the moment to bring to your consciousness, how human child development is a place where you must start in order to raise more human and humane adults."

74

Fine, except your emphasis on child rearing as a cause of social and global chaos seems extreme. This is not another Dr. Seuss story is it? Most adults are raised normal, successfully raised to become normal or we wouldn't use the word normal. Abnormal people are just a fact of nature.

"Not at all, in fact, manners of child rearing is a root cause of normality and abnormality as you call it. Scientists in Japan, the U.S., and France have given intense research into what is most essential to the optimal growth of the human brain after birth. Allan Schore's studies at the UCLA School of Neurology have compiled conclusions published in three major books. His findings show that a child without an attentive mother or surrogate parent does not develop the frontal right brain. The Right Brain contains all that we call human. A child can become severely handicapped both socially and in terms of intelligence without a mother's attention and interaction."

Isn't this the old controversy about the left and right hemispheres?

"It is no longer a controversy. Infants given close attention by the mother in the first three months of life, and then on a second level in the first three years, develop a superior intelligence to those infants who do not. Schore observes that the early development applies to the three major areas of the human brain from the cerebellum, through the limbic system, to the frontal lobes of the right brain, that the human brain grows faster on the right side than the left during this post-natal time. In the right portion of the human brain bears all those attributes which Terrans consider the most human characteristics."

So, what characteristics are those?

"Obviously, they are intelligence, creativity, the capacity to empathize, but most importantly, a concept of the Self as a secure entity."

It's a little hard for me to think of a human newborn as an 'entity'.

"Interesting, you think of us that way. Another author, Joseph Chilton Pearce cites other scientific studies that the impact of motherly warmth, caressing, and talk have beneficial effects absent in infants that receive none of that attention in the first forty hours after birth."

If that is the case, just think of what happens to unwanted children or children placed in children's homes and nurseries without ever seeing or being loved by their birth mother.

"Indeed. The consequences are immensely far-reaching in all mammalian life. Mother's or infant care givers are essential to an infant's potential brain and physiological development. Parents can give their child the best of detached care with well-trained 'nannies' and propel the child into right-brained learning modes like learning Mandarin Chinese by the age of two, and still produce a sociopath. If that early intimate relationship between mother and infant does not occur or exist, the child may appear quite normal, but may ultimately be a profound danger to any and all around them, void of the capacity for human empathy."

O.K. Now I think I am with you. I think you need to explain more about this. Realize the vast majority of parents consider themselves and their mode of child raising quite adequate.

"Undoubtedly they do, but without information available to them and with the intervention of the American medical profession as the scion of good advice, there is no consistency or agreement in the rearing of children. So, what a parent does have at his/her disposal is the model of how they were raised by their parents."

There are vast numbers of books on this subject, the famous Dr. Spock, for example. What is so new and profound that you even dwell on this subject?

"I need to inform you because in the absence of good parenting, something profoundly damaging happens. If you produce more narcissistic personalities or extremes of narcissism in the form of megalomania and sociopathy, it ultimately threatens the well-being of everyone on the planet. As more mothers are working in your profit-based society '*to make ends meet*,' as is said, their absence of awareness and availability to the infant is more common."

O.K., but what does a mother need to do to insure a healthy or an optimal child?

"Fortunately, for most humans, women naturally do the right thing, if for no other reason than by default. Most humans are right-handed. Therefore, they hold a baby in their left arm, while they do other things with their right hand."

I don't get it. Why does that make a difference
and what about left-handed mothers? Do they
raise less well developed children?

"Both naturally hold their infants in their left arm. What makes the difference according to Shore is the eye contact with the child and the attending cooing and smiling that goes on between mother and child, games played by the mother by turning her head away or leaving the room then returning. Her eye-contact or re-entering the room, all contribute to a sense of security and stability in the infant.

"Mother and child entertain each other's minds right-brain to right-brain. When the mother turns away, the child initially becomes upset, even secreting cortisol into its bloodstream, but with the return of the mother's face the child secretes happy-making brain chemicals (*serotonin*, *dopamine*, and *oxytocin*) that stimulate the happiness lobes of the brain. With such attention the affect of the child becomes calmer and more secure, its intelligence rises leading toward a more functional adult."

Not to get away from the main subject, but I
have known women, mothers, who were immensely attentive to their children, almost ob-
sessively so. That's normal from what I can
see.

"True, but any obsession manifests the mother's own stress and anxiety, which is felt by the infant and thereby neutralizing the potential for a happier response."

So what happens to a child that is deprived of
attention on a daily basis or given relatively indifferent attention as with a baby sitter, a

nurse, or nanny? Is this true just for Terrans
or is your specie subject to the same rules?

"TED, we love our children just like you. Yes, love and life equals sentience. Have you been to a zoo lately or have you seen penguins protect and nurture their eggs?"

O.K., understood.

"Finally, we arrive at the most important part. In the first three months of human life the right hemisphere of the human infant's brain develops two to three times as fast as the left hemisphere and larger in size. It does not mean the shape of the skull is affected, only the activity of those parts of the brain that light up with appropriate stimulation. Among the several developmental assets achieved in right brain development is the capacity to empathize with the external world, with people especially, but also with animals, the environment, and with various conditions."

So, what happens to a child who has little or no empathy? Can it be acquired later in life, if it isn't developed in those first three months or years?

"You love to ask two questions with every one. As I am sure you well know empathy is the ability to project oneself into the identity of another in terms of feelings or even an intellectual understanding. So, who would you believe might be a non-empathic personality?"

Somebody who doesn't care about other people, their feelings, or condition?

"So, again, what kind of person or profession would you expect someone to be non-empathetic?"

A surgeon?

"A surgeon could be very empathetic, since he realizes his patient has been anesthetized and is feeling no pain and therefore not suffering. On the other hand, dentists have the most difficult time with empathy since they can see and hear the patient when he feels pain."

I would think a butcher might need to be non-empathetic, a murderer, a serial killer, a rapist, someone who is put in charge of executions, someone who tortures.

"Now we are getting somewhere. So, what major professionals really need to be non-empathic?"

Lawyers (my wife's especially), judges, businessmen, generals, soldiers, politicians to be sure.

"Why do you think that is?"

Certainly I would include lawyers and judges because they are adhering to legal rules and precedent. Politicians who care nothing about the welfare of their constituency or the general public appear common place.

"For most of that list it might be important to assume one's psychological detachment from a person or event, but most humans are empathic and do feel compassion for others even when you disagree with them."

I believe that to be true. But how does a non-empathic person become a danger or a threat?

"You and we both have a descriptive term for someone who has no capacity to empathize, a 'sociopath.' Sociopaths tend to be narcissistic, indifferent to human pain and suffering, indifferent to threats to human life or the global environment. They usually have a hard time staying in relationships. They like to follow rules and often rigid and abusive to their children and wives. At the same time, they will betray their trust while demanding absolute devotion to the sociopaths' own conflicting and hypocritical values."

Yes, X, we see that all the time. It is easy enough to see every day violent abuses of women and children making the news. So, you would say these acts are more to do with child rearing than male testosterone and losing control?"

"No, its all of those things. But the sociopath can be extremely hurtful and harmful in their interactions without realizing it. He or she is usually contemptuous of other people who do have feelings, especially those who express them. The sociopath is preoccupied by signs and symbols, uniforms, everything being in its right place; otherwise, he feels the necessity to take stringent action *'to bring order to the chaos'* he sees all around him. What he does not see is the chaos or hypocrisy of his own thinking. Fundamental to the sociopath is obedience. Not obedience to any collective concepts, but those pertaining to himself and his position in the Vertical Order.

"Obedience is perceived as one of his most important virtues and he will do everything in his power to obtain submission and domination over anyone who does not fit his perceptions of absolute right and wrong. Rules take the place of what would be considered common sense to most human beings. Formality is preferred over casual. Whether it is couched in terms of 'Obedience to God' to hierarchical order, the hierarchy does not work in the sociopath's mind unless the subject conforms to absolute obedience."

It sounds like you are describing tyrants, despots, dictators and the like.

"Yes. Absolutely! But it also applies equally to a policeman making a command or an arrest. With authority assigned to the police, the requirement for obedience can apply to the least inconsequential comment or moment. If someone does not submit to absolute obedience, that person could be assassinated and the policeman making the command will be exonerated by the Vertical structure, regardless of how vile his act against the 'disobedient.' No "Great Religion" can tolerate any form of disobedience without consequences.

"Here is where we come full circle back to the delusion of an orderly society based on law, based on religion, based on hierarchy, based on absolutes, which in turn are based on authority."

Sociopaths must exist on every level of society.

"Of course they do. Without any understanding on the part of most human beings of how they can be effective and developmentally positive for their infant children, what else can be expected? On the other hand, any Vertical Social structure creates sociopathic thinking and acts in the name of the Vertical Order. If you look at people who call themselves 'conservative,' it could mean almost anything about anything. However, if there is a consistent pattern of sociopathy behind their 'conservatism,' the sociopath would be using this word as a covert disguise for his real nature.

"Look at your global history and the savagery of war, of abuse, of mass murder, indiscriminate violence. There you will see how the sociopath (often seen as a psychopath if negative attentions are directed at self, family, friends or local people). Tragic events and conditions merge and appear in such a way that the sociopath's personality seems acceptable and normal. Strangely, those catastrophic defects are even celebrated by the sociopath him/herself as crowning achievements and victories, even though the consequences are catastrophic to all involved."

But there are millions who support sociopathic leaders. What about someone who profits from war but whose main concern is with the acquisition of wealth? Are these sociopaths too?

"Tragically, you Terrans have glorified wealth in the form of money and property so greatly that you offer all kinds of rationalizations for corruption, gangsters, racists, and sociopaths of all kinds. As long as they are making a profit and paying some taxes, you have a hard time believing the depth of their profound illness, deceit and evil. Least of all can you trace such behaviors alone to motherhood or child rearing in general."

So, would you say that Vertical Society lends itself to sociopathy?

"Yes, I just said that. Vertical Society depends on sociopaths to enforce the hierarchical order. Look at who is at the top of Vertical hierarchies. If one is not sociopathic in a Vertical hierarchy, they either become sociopathic or put on all the vestiges of that condition. Someone can be trained to be a sociopath based on orthodoxy and dogma. Similarly, one can be trained to have empathy, but for the poorly reared child, it is a difficult task."

What about someone who is mentally ill, as opposed to a sociopath or psychopath?

"In a sane society psychopathy and sociopathy are mental illnesses. For example, when someone who is a schizophrenic hears voices telling him to kill someone for whatever reason, that person is going to do whatever the voices are telling him unless he can be calmed by medications. There are brain defects. SID (Sudden Infant Death) can be traced to a brain defect. Vertical Societies in their various forms provide the illness of mind as a legitimate and measurable component of a civilized society. The less empathic societies use the mentally ill to do things that they cannot ask or train an average person to do. You often refer to them as 'black ops' people or 'special forces' using people carefully identified as having no emotional or empathic responses to anything happening around them or precipitated by them."

> I don't think mothers have much to do with
> real mental illnesses, unless they abuse them-
> selves or their children.

"Unfortunately, parental abuse can come from so many causes it is difficult to say in each case where there seems to be mental illness in a parents' actions that bring about such a condition. That is not to dismiss the necessity of motherly touch, intimate contact with the child in the first three months of life, as we have discussed."

> I know that schizophrenia seems to show up in
> late puberty, over which parents usually find
> themselves in a situation they cannot control.
> It's more disconcerting when they feel they
> have done 'all the right things' as parents.

"It is truly difficult to put oneself in the mind of a schizoid child. The chief characteristic is that schizophrenics hear voices, they can be good voices, benign ones, or absolutely evil voices, but voices they do 'hear.'"

> How do we know they are hearing voices other
> than their telling us that is happening?

"Schizophrenics have been examined under the most stringent scientific conditions. What is an amazing result of these studies is that the part of the brain that receives and transmits sound becomes active and lights up during the 'auditory' illusion. Therefore, it is as real as the words on this page and your spoken word."

Does that mean anyone in history those who heard voices, divine or otherwise, were Schizophrenics?

"Quite possibly, after all, the voices are very real, just as real as our conversation. So, are you asking about other examples of auditory illusion in history?"

Yes.

"The distinguished Princeton professor Julian Jaynes, neurologist, discovered that when certain part of the human brain are stimulated with an electrode, the patient who is awake during the brain surgery describes a wide variety of phenomenon: A grandparent giving a command, a forgotten song sung by her mother as an infant is recalled word for word, note for note."

I can think of the most famous example, the Trojan War fought by the Greeks on Trojan soil. They could not seem to do anything without hearing a voice from the sky gods telling them what they should do to achieve victory over the Trojans.

"Yes, and Jaynes makes the same observation, but with the added insight that the other half of the so-called Legend of the Trojan war supposedly written by Homer, has no talking to the gods at all. They are silent. Odysseus must think rationally to get his ships and men back to the Greek mainland. Jaynes observes that a major transition occurs in the 800 years or so of the telling of those legends. In the absence of writing for that time, stories were told word for word by the best memorizers. Homer simply wrote down the legends of Troy and the Odyssey after nearly a thousand years of editing and conflations."

Didn't anyone notice the different in patterns of thought between the two parts of the Trojan Legends before Professor Jaynes?

"Apparently not! What this observation does is to set the human mind in a mode dominated by the left hemisphere of the frontal cortex. From that time on in Greek history the achievements of the Greeks are attributed to a rational approach to the external world. It was the basis of their conquest over the Persians who had brought a great army and navy to Greece initially succeeding in destroying nearly every city state including Athens. Using their capacities for reason, they devised ships, attacks, and schemes to defeat a much larger army than all the city states of Greece combined.

"After about a thirty-year period of grieving, saving the ruins as a testimony to the perfidy, irrationality and viciousness of the Persians, the Athenians rebuilt the High City (*acropolis*) in Athens using the most sophisticated technical methods and supreme aesthetic considerations to rebuild the Parthenon, the entrance gate, and the house of Erectheus, one of the ancient Myceneans who fought at Troy.

"From that time for decades they built a democracy and a city based on the intellect and genius of the Athenian people. It was their answer to divine kingship that dominated the Persian Near East. It's that recognition of their capacity to approach the world and their conflict with reason. Reason became the foundation of the ideals ultimately celebrated by those who composed the U.S. Constitution.

"These imitators of ancient Greece made an attempt to transit from a Vertical Society to a Holographic one, but because they did it by stealing money collected from other city states to fight the Persians, they got into a war with their neighbors the Spartans and Corinthians who had also won major victories against the Persians. Consequently, racked by war, the Democracy and the economies of Greece collapsed, although not its memory."

So, should I consider anyone who heard a voice or had a divine sign or intervention schizophrenic?

"Possibly. Just look at Moses, Abraham, and Jesus. Their voices were trying to convey positive messages: Moses because he heard the voice of God, saw a bush spontaneously ignite near him, and saw tablets of stone magically carved before his very eyes. Abraham's vision of the angel preventing him from slaying his son Isaac not only brought an end to the

84

magical sacrifice of Jewish tribes for a man's requirement to kill his first-born son. Animal sacrifices served the same function, often to guarantee continued good crops. Ultimately, this tradition provided the concept of symbolic sacrifice of one's son, a tribal model applied to God's sacrifice of his '*only son*' Jesus.

> Jesus spoke with God frequently, at times very troubled by his destiny and agony on the cross. His exclamation: '*Why have you forsaken me?*' is testimony for identifying Jesus as a schizophrenic, feeling he needed to sacrifice himself for all mankind, commanded by a 'divine' and absolutely authoritarian voice he called his '*father in heaven.*'

"His self-sacrifice continues the pre-Abrahamic practice that necessitates the father sacrifice his most beloved son. Abraham showed no mercy, that is, no empathy in obedience to his assumed dogma of Vertical requirements. Only divine intercession prevented him from killing his son. However, by divine intervention, he is simultaneously taught empathy and mercy, attributes up to that moment belonged exclusively to the divine, who having all human attributes, defy gravity, living somewhere in the heavens above."

> I never thought about Jesus in this way or the myth of divine intervention in the Abraham story. So, you must think this is a very important story about endowing humanity with the capacity to empathize even though he still lives under the commands of a dogmatic Vertical Society. It is also a story about empathy, divine or otherwise, as a chink in the block of Vertical absolutism.

"You really did get it this time TED! Schizophrenics often hear instructions to suicide in order to save somebody, or in Jesus case, to save all of mankind, as an expression of God's forgiveness similarly expressed in Noah's survival in the flood, the three Jews in the fiery furnace, and Abraham not executing his beloved son, Isaac. It would appear Jesus' to sacrifice himself was on a suicide mission, perhaps also an example of ADD or ADHD this time to save the '*sons of man,*' all Terrans from infanticide, child abuse, sending one's children to war, and ultimately Magical Thinking."

Where does someone find solace? None of us created this condition intentionally.

"That's why we're here now."

What can we do?

"Foremost, make sure every mother knows the importance of her participating with her infants in the first forty hours, the first three months, the first three years, and first seven of their lives. If the mother dies or fails to give this essential care, a surrogate must do so. Simultaneously, it becomes extremely important to identify and root out all sociopathic personalities from responsible positions of your hierarchies in all areas of life. One must omit all children from this separation as they will operate on any level, including sociopathy, having no 'executive function,' to make independent or moral decisions."

LOG IX

MONEY & "POWER OVER"

"Also, one of the second things you must do is to eliminate your monetary system."

What? What do you mean, X? That's impossible.

"Nothing is impossible. You must realize that everything about your present global system is about constraint and control."

You mean change it, don't you? I mean it is impossible to eliminate it. Money is the basis of exchange for all advanced societies.

"Oh, 'advanced' again. Remember I have been telling you your society is hardly advanced and more importantly, is in a constant state of fracturing and collapse. One measure of that is that you use money as a medium of exchange. Then you make it even worse by attaching all kinds of values to it like intelligence, talent, power, order, stability, personal worth, net worth, superiority, where money and its accumulation is little more than a measure of materialistic greed and self-delusion. You say things like *"If I were wealthy, I would have it all."*

So, what's wrong with that?

"Your monetary system of exchange is a source of your instability as groups, as individuals, to the point that people are killed for it or even commit suicide by such a perverted value system."

Wow. I cannot imagine a society without money. Yes, I admit it seems unfair at times, and there are really rocky economic times, but how could a moneyless society work? Give me a break, X. I am beginning to think I am not talking to an extraterrestrial entity but to an idiot cell in the right hemisphere of my brain.

"Peace TED. You say 'it seems unfair at times.' No, 'seems' only means that you know it is totally unfair, totally unfair at all times, but you can't admit it because you are so locked into this memory jacket, your *idée fixe*. Then you admit 'rocky economic times!' Your system of money is always rocky; better, it is like a hot coal sitting on a slab of ice in the middle of an ocean. It is a construct, an artificial construct and along with it all of the false and delusional values associated with it. In your system anyone who for whatever reason has more access to money, wealth, makes it less available to others. That is a fundamental premise of any monetary system. Wealth breeds poverty."

> Now you are losing me again. Wealthy people
> reinvest their money, create industries, and
> make a nation economically strong. They
> know how to bring benefits to many instead of
> the few.

"Do you believe that wealthy people are altruistic, that they want to help the rest of humanity?"

> Well, maybe not all of them, but most do.

"You are drinking the poisons of a profit-based society. Everything you just mentioned is self-delusion. Since your earliest civilizations you have stories about greed, greedy kings like Midas or greedy businessmen like Scrooge. Regardless of how silly these kinds of stories may be, they exist because they are red flags to how you Terrans can be so easily compromised."

> I wouldn't say compromised, but it is a give
> and take system.

"In your system, giving is given only to be retaken. Donations by the wealthy to this or that organization or purpose is always a Return On Investment (ROI). When the return is not obvious, you think of the donor as both wealthy and generous when, in fact, they are getting tax deductions and their wealth is never diminished by redistributing their wealth. It takes many forms. It might be getting one's name attached to a building a bridge or a branch of an institution, but there is always a return accompanied by many kudo's."

> Are you saying anyone with wealth is self-serv-
> ing and lacks any real generosity?

"No. Of course not, but almost. If we understood you Terrans to be permanently locked into inextricable mental frameworks and systems, we would not be having this conversation. It is essential for you to recognize that you belong to a vast universe; you are one among billions of evolved intelligent entities that exist. You minds are much more flexible (plastic is a term sometimes used) more plastic than you can imagine at most times in your history. That's why we are here, why I am talking to you. When you were a child you needed a parent, true?"

Yes, of course. So you are saying you are trying
to be an exo-parent?

"More like a graduate school mentor, who functions as *in loco parentis* for skills you develop."

Is your society moneyless?

"Yes, absolutely! It is a characteristic only of Vertical/pyramidal societies centered on a *civis*, a city, a Vertical "civilization." Centralization of wealth means centralization of authoritarian power. Just look at official architecture where the 'seats of power' lie. Those buildings are either fortresses (because the resident authoritarian knows his illegitimacy) or it has a dome crowning it as a metaphor for the vault of heaven and for divine dispensation of the authoritarian Vertical power holder. It is as artificial as any pyramid built on the planet. Pyramids are just metaphors for that centralization of authority around which mystagogic constructs are built to proclaim 'power over.'"

What do you mean, 'mystagogic' and 'power over?'

"Mystagogic is just exactly what it means: a system of thought that is based on mystery led by an individual who has access to understanding those mysteries and can teach them to others. In your ancient civilized societies, these are the priests, the shamans, sages, wise men, the seers who claim to have answers for the a-rational and strange, especially if they appear to be threatening or life-changing. In modern times they are the generals, politicians, and bankers. 'Power over' is also a self-induced human construct intended to offer protection from unknown events and entities that the average Terran would think of in that way."

Wait a minute. Isn't any civilization or organized society a 'construct' as you call it?

"Yes, the short answer is that there is order in the universe, a profound order, one you might call nature, and you
have yet to discover it. Instead, you have constructed a notion
of human social organization that is self-destructive and bar-
barically cruel. So divorced it is from the natural order of
things, you cannot see and are unwilling to admit how utterly
self-destructive your earthly entities are. For you randomness is chaos. Nature is random guided only by evidentiary
interlocking pieces, which you are beginning to reveal. Economy is the delusion of control, however a control of big versus
small. The nuances of economic exchange are not really understood for which reason it is always on the brink of collapse."

And you are saying this is all because of the
global monetary system we humans are inherently self-destructive and cruel?

"You always prefer to misunderstand me. Of course not!
What I am telling you is that the system is an artificial construct that rules out all other possibilities. If anyone should
threaten that construct by disbelief or rational thought, they
can expect to be routed out of the monetary and social system, or worse, slain."

Well, I think that if I told anyone that I had a
moneyless social system that would work better, no one would kill me. They'd just laugh or
call me a Communist.

"Yes, probably."

"Look, let's be reasonable for a moment. You must know
that if people are not rewarded, they would probably not do
anything, twiddle their thumbs, watch more television, play
golf, ping pong if they were lucky. Nothing that was excellent
or great would ever be done because there would be no motivation."

"To answer you about this kind of argument is so tire-
some I want to go to sleep. However, I asked for this encounter and will give you the briefest summary. Your brain is fried,
TED! Your name I gave you, TED, might better serve as an

anagram for Terminally Ensconced Dementia. Surely, you can think better than that!"

I've annoyed you, again!

"Not one whit. I knew what you were going to set before me from the beginning but I let you say it because it does mirror the slave mentality that has been instilled in the majority of Terrans as it carries with it the inherent hierarchy of Vertical/pyramidal systems."

O.K. I need to ask a seemingly stupid question, but when you use 'hierarchy' I need to ask what do you mean?

"Not stupid at all. A hierarchy is the essence of the flimsy fabric of a Vertical/pyramidal system based on the exchange of wealth and power. Your English word hierarchy derives from two Greek words, *hieros* and *archos*, or *archon*, translated, means holy power, or holy old men who rule. What hierarchy means in a Vertical Society is whoever is at the top of the Vertical pinnacle is necessarily considered holier and wiser than the rest of humanity and that the source of their holiness and authority is intrinsically, inherently, hereditarily, genetically dispensed but always divinely given.

"Inversely, the more elevated one is in human society, the more likely that person will assume divinity. He or she will perceive his/her divine appointment as a delusional pretext at the very best. All of the attributes, signs and symbols of authority, power, holiness or divinity, are intended to enshroud the apex of this Vertical structure. It takes all forms, be they costumes, ceremonies, ritual acts, treasures in stone and gold, ostentatious and supportive, mirroring subsystems--often utterly absurd ones. Each cloaks the fragility of the Vertical pyramid or cone and all of its claims and delegations of authority from the delusional fantasies and foppish nonsense they are."

You may be making a good case for seeking an alternative to Vertical/pyramidal systems, but haven't these kind of systems always existed, even in the earliest human art and hunting tools dating back to the Paleolithic Age? And another question: without a monetary system don't you just have a barter system or gift giving? Something so simple could not ever support a global economy or city planning, infrastructure, mass production of material goods, and the like?"

"Certainly not for both questions, as in a humanely designed society there is no bartering. I wish you would ask just one question at a time because every answer demands multiple levels of explanation. Before I tell you any more about a non-monetary society, I think I need to go back in your history and give you a broader perspective than the one you obviously held."

That's unnecessary. I know enough history to say that over the millennia human life has improved, that we are no longer savages, that we do not worship idols, we have a science and technology that man has never had before. While it may make life more complicated, it is much easier to survive. We also have educational systems that improve all of those things. More has been understood, revealed, developed, and printed in the last 20 to 25 years than in all of the rest of known human history.

"TED you have just proven to me that I do need to give you a bigger picture. Please take no offense."

LOG X

HOLOGRAMS OF HUMAN LIFE ON PLANET EARTH

"Let me assure you that while you have many thoughts based on your social envelopment in the form of maxims, clichés, stereotypes, and prejudices, I can tell that you have instinctively thought beyond these limitations, but still have no firm footing in reality. Rather than flopping about in your septic confusion, I want to offer you a simple framework in which to simplify human history and put a little island of knowledge beneath your feet that you will eventually come to welcome."

With all due respect, I welcome that, but is this going to be another long lecture?

"Patience, my friend, please! No. I will make it as simple and brief as possible. Would you not agree that humans think in space-time relationships?"

I suppose. Mathematicians say that there are possibly as many as eleven dimensions to the universe; in fact, Michio Kaku once said 'God is mathematics.' I understand we live in a three-dimensional world in time, so four dimensional....

"Good! That is an oversimplification, but it demonstrates what I want to do with you right now; think abstractly, as abstractly as you just described your physical world as you understand it."

O.K. I can do that.

"Millions of years ago there was an intervention by what you call 'extraterrestrials' in the total obliteration of one of your solar circumnavigating planets. You know it as the so-called asteroid belt, once the fifth planet from the sun. When this great catastrophe occurred, it affected every planet in your solar system, fragments of the destroyed planet striking your moon, the earth, and all the planets in the solar system. Still, today, your scientists have recognized an anomalous variable pointing to a missing planet, but cannot find it. Some say it is the effect of a second sun; some say it is the impact of exploding stars elsewhere in the galaxy, which is actually partially correct, but primarily, it is the disintegration of that fifth planet."

I am aghast, speechless really. Was there life
on that planet?

"If the legends of many galactic societies are correct, yes."

But you said it was caused by an intervention
of 'extraterrestrials,' so why is it just a legend?

"Because it dates so far back in time, perhaps even a billion earth years back or as recently as the last known earthly Extinction Event twenty-million earth years ago. More important is the reason. The Terrans of that planet had, like yours, discovered the nuclear components of matter and had developed weapons like your people have done, then having discovered some of the materials and techniques of inter-galactic flight; they posed a great risk to the other intelligent entities in this galaxy."

So, they got into a war with the 'extraterrestrials' of that time and got blown up?

"You are thinking of General McArthur's statement that the next Great War would be fought in outer space."

No, I didn't know he said that.

"Anyway, it is much worse than that, dating long before we formed intergalactic alliances and developed certain framework for rules of inter-galactic conduct such as our mutual non-intervention with other planets in the galaxy, relations were one-on-one."

But you are talking to me. Doesn't that violate
this treaty of non-intervention?

"Ah, you are quick. No. No, because we have a long-term investment in you and we have a form of galactic approval."

Now you claim you are investing in us. Isn't
that monetary?

"No, Not at all. It is only that we are more invested in Terrans because we, among several other coalition members, have intervened to change your DNA in such a way that you will not seek an interplanetary war and might find the peace and happiness that has escaped you for the last six to ten thousand years of what you call 'civilization.'"

So, you are manipulating us. Isn't that 'power over,' as you call it?

"No. It means we have intervened to change your DNA and because we over looked some inherent flaws, and must do it again."

Again? I don't think I want to ask how you are going to do that.

"Good, we can continue with the quick summary of human social development that led to all the wonderful benefits you claim to enjoy. Our last Terran intervention occurred quite by accident about 90,000 earth years ago. Partly out of a lapse of interest, we failed to remove some plasma from the sun. It was going through one of its major cycles of solar flares like the minor ones that occur about every 13,000 years caused by galactic super waves, phenomenon that are part of all galactic instabilities. Anyway, a series of flares occurred which scorched half of the planet, creating an intervention by default instead of intent, thanks to our negligence."

Do you mean that the earth and its inhabitants are like a nursery remotely guided by an alien civilization? You are parenting us all along, like you said earlier?

"Why is that so surprising. Many earthlings have believed that for centuries and some still do. Did you forget '*God and all His angels?*' It is more like mentoring rather than parenting, although the latter is sometimes necessary."

It's not so surprising if you put it that way.

"The positive outcome of that forgetfulness on our part was that the surviving humans discovered their sun had a life of its own and on occasion could punish the earth made it an object of reverence. At least that was how mass death and destruction was understood at that time when solar bursts occurred. While it was a healthy assumption, it led to cults of the sun and deification of virtually all the stars and constellations in the nighttime sky. More importantly, under the stress of that changed environment, humans realized they had to think of ways of protecting themselves and using more of the left hemisphere of the brain than in past millennia, not that they had a conscious choice."

X, you are saying we can adapt to our environment by virtue of our brains, our thoughts.

"Yes, absolutely. It is one of the reasons that we have as much hope in you as we do."

Is this a kind of validation of Darwin's evolution of the species?

"You could say that, but Darwin has been validated enough. If I may continue?"

Wait, please! You said you, your civilization, over-looked removing plasma from the sun in order to protect us from solar flares and 'galactic super waves?'

"Yes, our people do not do that extraction but others have succeeded who evolved with a hot sun nearby or two suns. They do that service...drawing plasma from the sun. Why are you looking so strangely?"

My God! You must know that this year, 2013, NASA's project to constantly film the sun recently captured a giant sphere near the surface of the sun, probably many times the size of the earth and that it seemed to be drawing a column of hot plasma from the sun into itself. Not only that, but after it left the sun, a great turbulence of fiery plasma swirled around on the sun's surface as if the surface itself was disturbed somehow by the object having poked a hole in the sun.

"Yes, I am aware of it, but consider also that a dark circle, possibly a sphere, was filmed extracting the plasma from the sun. It means that it also sucked in all the peripheral light of the sun near that disk or sphere, otherwise the NASA cameras could not have documented the apparent spherical shape."

You mean the sphere was functioning something like a black hole, so powerfully dense that even the sun's light could not escape from it? If that were the case, how could it be so close to the sun and not be vaporized or even sucked into the sun itself? After all, the density of the sun has many times the mass of all of its planets, or could it be a function of NASA's camera lens?

"Correct. Let's leave those questions to GE University, Physics 101. It is a fairly common occurrence when a sun begins to make major flares. There is always a danger that it could collapse and explode destroying any life on surrounding planets or simply consume them. Your sun is not predicted to do that for another billion years, however."

You say 'when "a" sun makes major flares,' it must mean you are monitoring other suns?

"Yes, but let's get back to the subject. You recall our mapping out the Planar and Vertical Societies."

Yes, so, what did the Yale professor call the third phase?

"He didn't. Perhaps he was too early, but others have identified this third phase as the "molecular" society, the "nuclear" society, but I prefer your Star Wars term 'holographic,' meaning the social structure is based on an interwoven, integrated form, recognizing technological, scientific, and humanistic integrations."

So, how is that better than a Vertical-Place centered society?

"It is neither better nor worse. It just is, as are all societies in all time. It is a better method of description in either simple or more complex societies. The journey from Planar to Vertical is a radical change if you make that distinction. More importantly it is a change that necessitates new synapses, new thinking, which humans are very reluctant to experience and usually perceive as a threat."

Interesting. I understand that to be applied to our society, I mean global society. We are all connected by phones, the Internet, cars, planes, and trains. Our advanced education systems teach many languages, many different traditions, histories, and we can see the remnants of our past through digitized images of art and architecture. We may not be unified as a planet, but we are connected more than at any time in human history.

For me the most holographic thing that has occurred in my lifetime is the Internet, but that interconnectedness was here with the telephone, telegraph, paved highways, steam engines, the combustion engine, aircraft, all of which have brought the most distant parts together.

"Yes, your simile to describe your connectedness is totally appropriate. However, I want to suggest an even more profound interconnectedness."

The environment!

"Excellent thought but even more interconnected than that is your human brain. It is what you Terrans need the most, take care of the least, and do not fully treasure in other human beings on the planet. Your brain is a 3-4 pound piece of mostly wrinkled clumps of fat and oxygen bearing blood vessels, with electro-chemicals making billions of synaptic connections whether you are asleep or awake. Nevertheless, it is one of the universe's miraculous products."

So, you are saying we are already holographic beings, I presume like you, or somewhat like you, since I still don't know what you look like.

"Now we jump from the brain to the body. O.K. We are all holographic beings in a holographic universe. We are all made of essentially the same stuff. What you or I look like is unimportant. We share the same universe, the same physics, the same in so many ways that how we look is unimportant. An informed person is not a frightened person, least of all crippled by fear. Fear is essential to Vertical/Place social structures and utterly meaningless in or to holographic systems."

Don't you think that we have good reason to fear the Four Horsemen of the Apocalypse: malnutrition, disease, war, and death?

"Only the last is relevant to a Holographic Society and that is something unworthy of fearing."

> You mean a Holographic Society eventually solves the problems of hunger, disease, and war?

"Are we not proof?"

GAMES HUMANS PLAY

> Before you answer that, I just want to say that human beings are doing better with regard to the first three horsemen.

"Apologies! Although you have holographic brains and holographic thinking on some technological and social levels, your embedment in the Vertical Social structure is so profound that you need help. The famous 'Church father,' Augustine of the Roman Christian church, wrote that Jesus came *in the time of the greatest need.*' Yes, he did. This time you have a whole lot of Jesus's and it is they collectively who need to show up.

"You not only have millions of non-terrestrial visitors coming but you have the equivalent of a Jesus kind of personhood inside of each one of you. You have the capacity to think rationally, to love, to be connected with others, a desire to be acknowledged, a desire to be free, to freely make a positive contribution to the human condition. Once you learn how to raise a child, everyone will be able to empathize without any superficialities of sentimentality, the gruel of Vertical civilization."

> You really believe in us don't you? You must think we can make it through this transition from a Vertical to a Holographic Society. But what do you mean 'millions of non-terrestrial visitors coming? That scares the crap out of me.

"Yes we do have that understanding of you, as your pattern of history has occurred throughout the galaxy and others. Otherwise, why have this conversation? I have to modify that concern for you. We have a directive to protect all life, including you humans. As for the millions, they are observing for the most part from afar."

> How can we overcome the constraints and limitations of our global structures without creating absolute chaos? And I'm not sure I

like being seen through a looking-glass, so to speak.

"Think differently. You are already living in chaos, do you not see that? Your populations are growing in numbers and in ever-increasing poverty. You are in the midst of endlessly changing ideological and religious wars. You have political systems that do not work and never will because they are based on delusional, hierarchical, Verticalized thinking.

"Your society attempts to prove that it is the ideal society because you can have fun and material possessions once the exclusive privileges of kings and princes that most others on your planet still do not have. Fun and gathering material possessions is just childish play, lacking all responsibility. Rich men accumulate wealth at the expense of everyone else on the planet, which you are made to think is the way things are supposed to be. Rich men play golf, certainly one of the most thoughtless boring games among many you have thought up. It is a luxury game, hitting little balls, someone else's balls into little holes."

Sorry, I don't get it.

"Don't think there are no metaphors here. Poor people watch more violent games, rationalizing they are 'action centered,' but they are really about controlled pugilism and surrogates for thinking they have achieved something. The poorer the individual, the more compelled to participate and watch, create, and play more violent games. Having filled their spare time with delusional battles where the false hero always wins. Your preoccupation with battle games is about the silent rage the poor feel in view of their disempowered role in society."

Come on! These video games are games of skill, X. They are analogous to the hunt which humans had to do for thousands of years to survive. Not only that, they have rules, lest a temper or irrational violation of a rule occurs. There are referees, like judges, who enforce the rules of the games. They're not examples of degeneracy.

"Haven't said they are. Yes, skill is involved in any game, but so it is in all things including murder, mass murder as in war, but most of your games are about two things: one, they are anti-gravitational, because you are prisoners of gravity even with planes and rockets, and some reverse-engineered space vehicles; and two, because they are metaphors of 'power over.'"

Again, what do you mean 'power over?'

"Just that. If you win over an opponent, you have a victory, correct?"

Yes, that's what all games are about. What do your people do just play brainiac games like chess?

"Chess? No, certainly not. Chess is a game of victory in the name of kings and queens and other members of a medieval Vertical hierarchy. Have you ever thought about what the word victory means?"

Sure. I can't give a dictionary definition but it is about winning or struggling through something difficult and still coming out O.K. No, it means coming out ahead.

"Ahead of What? Winning and Victory are two different things. Victory describes the overwhelming conquest of one or more opponents. Militarily, and on many corporate and legal levels, it means complete subjugation of an opponent. Subjugation is 'power over.' Subjugation or annihilation is a form of mass destruction or enslavement."

Football and hockey games are contact sports. Call them violent if you want, but there are rules of control. A defeated football team does not become 'annihilated' or 'enslaved.' What nonsense!

"Absolute nonsense, for sure! 'Winning' is just an empty metaphor for rape and annihilation."

O.K. I get it. You are trying to show me that games are just metaphors for 'power-over' played globally in Vertical manifestations of authority. Right?

"Yes, you are making progress."

I was being sarcastic.

"Unfortunately, your games are also metaphors of all conflicts, of ideologies against ideologies, religions against religions, disputes over the domination of territories, but especially of men against women and every level of sexual differentiation in between, from discrimination against manly women and womanly men, to forcible aggression and rape by males against females, bullies over the vulnerable."

So, you're saying love between women and
men is irrelevant?

"No, only your question is irrelevant. In Vertical Societies there is a constant, never-ending struggle, for placement in the Vertical hierarchy, as much of it operates unconsciously as it is conscious. Males like to take credit for forming the Vertical structure, be it a hill-top fortress, or a giant investment firm and then imposing and enforcing the Vertical structure, usually with brute, economic, male-based strength, legal, or cyber battles. Whether we are looking at a social hierarchy or a vertically constructed building, (church bell towers and *campanile* included) it does not matter. If the male is a police officer, a judge, a 'breadwinner,' or a referee at one of your 'games,' their role is about domination through power-over."

How can you say that? We have female police,
good judges. Not only that, women in the US
bring home 70% of a family income. They are
truly female 'breadwinners.'

"'Bully, bully for you.' Without a doubt currently updated on the statistic, even though females are underpaid and often taken advantage of in a variety of ways by their 'superiors.' In 2012 over 26,000 cases of molestation or rape occurred in your military whose entire reason for existence is domination and power-over. There are too many examples of male domination in Vertical Societies to count. What we would like you to realize is that male domination is an all-pervasive condition of any Vertical Society. It is not an intentional construct of Vertical Society, but a natural consequence for which there are many consequences—a carry-over from two-dimensional hunting and gathering Planar cultures."

You mean there's more?

"Let's take your ball games, all of which are dominated by men, by the way. Is it so difficult to see men's ball games as feats of anything other than inseparably bound to maleness of one kind or another?"

No, not difficult! That seems almost too obvious. Most games have to do with the biological differences between men and women.

"We are not talking about whether a game is for men or women, even if you agree that ball games are dominantly male games. More importantly, it is the object of the game that creates an image of 'victory,' 'conquest,' and 'power-over.'"

Then, that is also just a function of male testosterone, right?

"Again, you are slipping away from the object of the game. Let's consider how you would think of the ball or hockey puck as less a metaphor for a contest of winning or not winning. Let's take American football as a metaphor for male domination over females, even as a violation and domination over the feminine?"

I don't get that at all. In fact it seems downright un-American. Women like football too.

"Let's try a thought exercise. Let's break for a moment your preconceptions about football, American style. Think of the actual American football itself as a female egg."

This is ridiculous.

"It's oval, not spherical, but don't let that destroy the simile. In your football games doesn't the Center hike the ball from between his legs into the hands of a specialist carrier or passing quarterback who is reaching under the Center's buttock to give birth to the play?"

Birth! Birth? What?

"Isn't the point of American football to keep the egg-ball from getting into the hands of the other team's males?"

It's not an egg! You mean the Center is giving
birth? That's obscene! I don't like this thought
exercise.

"Isn't the ball, kicked and passed around with great unconscious satisfaction to the observers in the grandstands as
well as to the players as they hit, push, grab and tackle each
other? Isn't it possible it is kicked, knocked, thrown into the
vaginal net in basketball or ice hockey, or between the raised
legs of the goal post of the opposing team, thereby violating
their opponents possession of the ultimate female puden-
dum? Don't you see? In each case, they are violating the other
team's 'woman.' A football victory is a kind of ceremonial
rape, in fact."

My god! I can't think of football that way. I
think you have just ruined all of my joy in
watching football.

"Or perhaps I have broken through the matrix of your
Vertical, male-dominated thought processes a little?"

Oh, my god. I should have known there would
be a price to be paid by talking to an EBE!

"Be at peace. There is more, because until you realize
how the by-products of Vertical Society work, you will be a
victim of its consequences."

Like what?

"Just give me some examples of social structures that
reflect male domination."

O.K. You have got to be male to have a family.

"Didn't you leave someone out?"

What I mean is if you are a father, a man will
take care of his wife and child. Correct?

"So, what you are telling me is that human males who
share their sperm with a woman and that union produces a
child, a real man has to be responsible for them?"

Yes. In our culture at the present time.

"So, in what ways does a male prove he is a man?"

Well, the obvious thing a male does as a man
is to protect and care for his wife and children.
I think some men think that the more children

they have the more male they are. Participating or watching sports, shooting guns, hunting, those are things men do together, traditionally without women. Protecting his country, too, if necessary. That's a big one. Being successful at what he chooses to do as work, that's a measure of man.

"All of that sounds quite male-ish. So, if a man goes off to war, does that make him a 'hero,' as everyone is told by people in the U.S. mass media, rallying behind the troops and vets?"

Hero is a pretty strong word. Some may be more heroic than others, but they seem more like victims to me than heroes. They did volunteer, however, at least since the Vietnam war after which they stopped drafting people.

"So, if they are 'victims,' then why would they volunteer? Does volunteering to face death make them more of a man, a hero, no less? And, yes, men enter the military knowing they may be gruesomely wounded or die, and that is possibly an act of male bravery or folly."

Lots of reasons, economic, promises of education, a career in the military, or a career in some other field. Some can earn citizenship by volunteering.

"Yes, so why do young men volunteer to put themselves in harm's way? Is it because men are supposed to be brave?"

Yes, of course. I left that out. Men consider being brave a virtue, a part of being a man...'Home of the free and the brave,' you know.

"Why do you suppose most males who volunteer are officially between the ages of 18 and 27?"

I suppose because you cannot legally join before age 18, and after 27 you are probably not as physically fit.

"This age range is also an age of immaturity for the male brain. His frontal lobes do not develop as quickly as they will for women for which reason he cannot make good decisions, lacking, as he does, what psychologists call *'executive judgment.'*

"'Executive judgment' is that capacity to not follow the crowd when something is potentially dangerous or unwise. Why do you think you are considered a 'minor' until age 21? You are not allowed to purchase alcohol. Correct? An exception is made for when you are allowed to vote at 18. Conversely, because the male brain is less developed than the female, he is more likely to be successfully trained to be obedient, even to the point of walking directly into gunfire, minefields, and exploding artillery. All armies use those who are lacking 'Executive Judgment,' the more violent use tweens and teens just for that reason."

> You mean, the male human brain hasn't fully matured until that late in life? Since most people did not live past 27 in the ancient world and European Middle Ages, it's a wonder the human race has survived.

"A wonder, indeed! So, what is the benefit for young men in this age group to volunteer, to put life and limb at risk? What is so male or heroic about that?"

> Nothing. I think it's the uniforms. If you have a uniform, you belong to a group and that group has a purpose, a very difficult one, a noble one, and that is the reason it is manly to join any military group. Once as a kid in 1943, only six years old, I saw some Marines marching in their dress uniforms. I told my mom I wanted to be a Marine. Also, for parents, I think that after several years of raising teenagers they are hoping sometimes the military will teach them self-discipline and that, too, seems to be a manly virtue...once it is achieved. If you are wounded or psychologically survive the terrors of killing and being wounded, men must feel heroic.

"Even though you didn't know about executive judgment, you clearly recognize that boys at those ages have a tendency to be undisciplined and not well self-regulated. So, why do you think that is?"

Raging hormones, I suppose.

"Exactly. It is during these ages that males reach their peak sexuality. They don't know much about sex, intimacy, or managing their sexual appetite. Least of all do they know anything about anything.

"What do boys and young men like to do during this time in their lives?"

Athletics, showing physical prowess, playing war games on their I-Pods together; learn all the names of cars that are 'cool'; talk about females, shoot guns, or play video guns, get illegal fire crackers around the Fourth of July, New Year's Eve, and for some, Christmas, any thing that explodes or makes a big noise is exciting to boys that age. Also, to do things not approved of by parents or society at large, like testing drinking alcohol and smoking; testing girls on how far they will go is major. Testing parents is big. Abusing anyone who does not seem to have fully transited from boy or girl to man or woman, especially gays. Verbal abuse is directed at anyone outside the norm of their own small group; playing sports is like you said, very common.

"Quite a long list, I'd say. Now we are back to testosterone, immature brains, and ball games, don't you think?"

It is, and everyone is glad when years of puberty are over.

"When the immature human brain meets floods of testosterone neither manly hair, an adult voice, nor a penis has been fully commissioned. The human male identity and sense of self can only be substituted by all of these things that go boom, that look like hardened penises such as knives, bayonets, guns, bullets, rockets. All of those phallus-like pointy things become surrogates for the absence of a full sense of self and power over all the awkwardness's and humiliations of a teen."

> We did talk about sex a lot. One of the younger kids didn't believe us when we were talking about how babies were born. We used to take my Dad's twenty-two rifle and pistol out to the canyon to shoot at bottles and cans.

"Just think, a high-powered automatic military style weapon is a machine spewing bullets like a penis ejaculating billions of spermatozoa. A powerful sleek automobile becomes a symbolic phallus and its shining and pointed surfaces a well-lubricated phallic shaft as psychologists proved for the automobile industries back in the 1950's. After intensive research, they discovered it was the nubile teenagers of families who most frequently determined the choice of an auto.

"So, now, TED, what conclusions can you make about young men joining the military?"

> Obviously weapons and some cars are images of power to powerless teenagers and impotence of nubile youth. Maybe some parents who want them to get the hell out of the house push them into the military. Maybe they were drafted, maybe it was not their fault.

"Images are very much substitutes for the Unrealized Self. For some males who never resolve their inner conflicts between reason and passion, the pubescent dilemma continues late into life, often to the detriment of a man's wife and family, especially if he is in a position of authority. Men often abuse their authority in surges of testosterone or blind stupidity based on their self-image of their position in Vertical Society. You have so many public examples in political positions, the police, and among some celebrities."

> Yeah, just look at the politicians who betray their wives, athletes who cheat by taking drugs, men who abuse their authority as school-teachers. So, while I appreciate your point about youth, so many men have not been

able to abandon their pubescent nature, 'Centaurs all,' one might say. Most older men today would be happy to get any part of "*four hours*" from the blue pill. We, as males, have a tough time.

LOG XII

GALACTIC EXCHANGE

I've been thinking.

"Again? I'm pleased to hear that."

If the Vertical Society constructs hierarchical values in all aspects of our earthly life, it would seem impossible to change to any other system. You claim you live in a Holographic System but I cannot see how that works. There have to be hierarchies of values; otherwise you have a Communistic system.

"Labels again! Dispose all your labels. They exist only as a means of simplifying complexities into stereotypical formulas, which when examined make no logical sense. Swearing for example is just an avoidance of making a more rational deciphering of something that has evoked rage. Moreover, among the galactic societies we have nearly all abandoned monetary systems of exchange, a major source of anxiety, rage and violence in your society. We're discussing something real, that already exists, tens of thousands of times over throughout the galaxy and probably in others."

As much as you have attempted to explain to me a holographic monetary system, I still cannot comprehend what that looks like other than outright theft, or a barter system.

"It is not a 'holographic monetary system.' It is simply not monetary, but there are values of exchange."

So, how could that be any different from our earthly system? What do you use in place of money?

"This is a barrier you Terrans are going to have to transcend on your own. Just a few questions: you mentioned theft. Theft, piracy, ownership, control all represent a tyrannical side of Vertical Society."

If we are talking about money in the Vertical Society, yes?

"Perfect. Now consider the opposite, if you can."

'Free everything' would mean no control and inevitable chaos.

"How quaint! Let's just take the first part of your answer, 'free everything.' Let's imagine for a moment that all food is free."

Really! Free food! I think we would end up with an even fatter society than we already have, for one thing. Gluttons would feast, sleep, poop, have sex, and then stuff their faces again. Great model for kids, right? God, the world population would explode! By the way, how populated is your planet of origin?

"Around 27 billion."

You see, that's exactly what happens!

"Much of our population live in exo-planetary systems and our planet of origin (PoO) is larger than yours, as well, accommodating large populations. Aside from that, we, like the animal world of your planet, we eat only out of necessity."

You really mean you do not have fat foods, fast foods, and junk foods?

"As a matter of fact, we do not."

Well, if beer and wine are part of your diet, you must have a lot of alcoholics.

"Very few people are ever found in inebriated or drugged conditions."

You know I am thinking '*What a boring society*,' but I know better than to assume you haven't solved the problem of scarcity and nourishment for your biology's.

"Yes, correct twice over."

You're playing with me, aren't you?

"A little. So what do you think I am conveying to you by suggesting we have no junk foods, that our people are well-nourished, not gluttonous, and have no problems with obesity, drugs, or alcohol?"

On Star Trek they had designer foods dispensed to them by machines.

"There you go. Star Trek again! At least someone was trying to think ahead. Your astronauts and cosmonauts have such EME's as do your 'soldiers in the field.'"

O.K. I'm a little embarrassed about my answer. You have probably solved all of the problems of appetite suppression and hunger by means of genetic disposition and adjustments to DNA.

"Well that's a helluva lot better than the Star Trek explanation."

But it also looks like a totally controlled, tyrannical, black-lunch-box society. Someone has to grow food, process it, package it, and maintain the machines that are built to do those things.

"At first sight, it might look that way."

Does this mean you have slaves?

"If you want to call machines slaves, yes."

So, doesn't anyone do any work?

"Millions, billions."

But how are they compensated?

"I just suggested one of the ways, free nourishment, and the total absence of scarcity and the guarantee of health."

So, who pays for that? Who designs and builds the machines that process the food, build the buildings for factories where that work is done, where the food is then stored and private dwelling places?

"Everyone works, as you call it. Like you, we see benefit in contributing to the social order and enjoy working in whatever occupation or skill is of interest to a person. Since we do not need food in the form of massive food production and are properly nourished, we do not have to 'earn a living,' as you call it in order to meet your fundamental biological needs for nourishment."

Dining is such a pleasure for humans. We love to eat. It is as much a social event as a necessity. Our economy depends on food and the infinite presentations of it. It's also a social thing whether for family, celebrations, friends, even eating something after a funeral. Food is a sign of life and renewal. One scientific study declared that eating is the single most satisfying experience humans have. It has more importance than fear, lack of water, and other human needs.

"As it is for virtually every specie in the known universe at one time or another. It becomes less imperative as there are no such things as holidays or weekends except for rites of passage."

Your advanced civilization is sounding more boring by the second.

"It would take humans a little adjusting. However, your transformed Holographic Society might look quite different from ours. The nature of that adjustment is owed primarily to the embedded Vertical idea that there must be scarcity, that dining with family and friends is the privilege of the wealthy who control scarcity and do not suffer from it. In a moneyless system there is no scarcity."

If there is no scarcity, then everyone has an equal chance for proper nourishment and do not have a need for money to exchange for food. Am I right on that?

"Yes, that's correct. It also means that with education from early childhood about health, gluttony is rare and easily treated when it occurs. Imbalanced diets are virtually unknown. As for boring, we have access to foods from all over the galaxy. What could be more exotic?"

What about utilities, energy?

"In order to have interstellar travel, the energy problem must be solved first and usually is soon after their solar planets become aware of nuclear power. Once that occurs, domestic needs for infrastructure become immensely simplified. Energy is in virtually endless supply and inexpensive to produce and use. Nuclear power being the most expensive for the simple reason there are no safe places to store nuclear processed radioactive materials. Then, Terran systems search for alternatives that do not threaten all life on their planets.

"Please recognize that as long as there are entities that control your current energy systems for profit, you will be in an energy crisis. Your 'energy people' all claim they have the best form of energy and cheapest available, but deliberately create 'scarcity' to drive up profits, and ignore discoveries like those of Mr. Tesla to keep the population ignorant and paying for something that is available and their right without payment.

"In a Holographic Society, there is no need to pay for anything but the energy generators, which become ubiquitous as obtained just as freely as food. You are not aware of it but energy is everywhere in and around you. The universe is constantly creating energy and movement and recreating it, most ostensibly in the form of life."

> So who makes those energy generators? Energy is our most urgent problem. That's why we have some many ways of capturing it. So who gets it for your society?

"Not who but what. Your stomach, machines, movement on sub-atomic levels. Energy is everywhere. You just do not want it unless it is profitable to the few whose interest is only that and not about producing energy on any and all sensible levels."

> But what about housing? How do you pay for that or build shelters of any kind as they more than any other kind of building require a lot of man hours no matter how simple the habitat?

"We found 'ownership' to be useless in a Holographic Society. Everyone lives in planetary cities, somewhat equivalent to apartments, but in single buildings each capable of supporting ten to 100 million per unit. Some of our galactic ships support similar populations"

> But how are people paid for the skills they acquire and professional knowledge?

"All housing is free as is all education. Our planetary cities are like very large spaceships, and our spaceships are self-sustaining inter-galactic space cities."

Still X, how are people compensated? Are there no rewards for anything? What keeps an alcoholic from drinking himself to death, or someone who loves expensive chocolates from eating them until they get Type-2 diabetes? Isn't a surgeon who saves lives more deserving of a greater compensation than a laborer building one of your super-cities?

"No, they are equal. We are compensated by our state of health. One's physical and psychological health is the single most important benefit to any social order. Without health the mind falters or becomes dysfunctional. Yes, for most there are rewards, but not appropriated by scarcity or need in the Holographic structure."

I'm stunned! How do you measure psychological and biological health?

"Those are all skills of what you call the medical profession. The only requirement is for a medical check-up after so many planetary days, whether residing on and in our planets of origin, or residing on a spaceship or a planet in another solar system. Our medicine is scientifically based and adjusts DNA when necessary for optimal psychological or biological well-being. As a result, we spend less on medical conditions per annum for 27 billion people than spent in the U.S. on medicine on 320 million people in a solar year. If you do not already know, your health system based on profit is the poorest among the industrial world creating an increasingly unhealthy population, no, a profoundly ill populations. We also outlive you by about 300 to 500 years."

So, how old are you X?

"As with your society, it is not polite to ask, but old enough."

I think I need to rest a little. You understand probably better than me. This is the Methuselah effect maybe, or was Methuselah also an EBE, a GE?

LOG XIII

MAGICAL AND HOLOGRAPHIC THINKING

I am tired. I can't sleep. It's really late. X, where are you?

"Here."

Good, at least I think so.

"You have a lot of unanswered questions, but before you share your confusion, I want to clarify your thoughts on work and compensation."

That's a relief, because it is inconceivable how a moneyless economy could possibly work. People need acknowledgement in terms of pay. It amounts to esteem humans feel providing for one's family, contributing to society, their profession, or just their hard work.

"Just know that for billions of thoughtful, intelligent beings in this galaxy and elsewhere, there is no need for monetary compensation when all other biological and social needs are met."

But what happens to individual creativity, pursuits of excellence in any field of endeavor without motivation? Most of all, what does a moneyless society have to do with health and well-being? How do you put a value on that?

"We put the greatest value on the individual who can contribute syncretically, biologically, intellectually, because like us, you are a hologram. Your relationship to your health and well-being are holographically bound to everyone on your planet of origin and to everything in the universe. Your creativity, your aesthetic values, your focused energy on so many questions affects the whole universe."

I would like to think that...the whole universe?

How am I a hologram?

"How did you get here? Did you will yourself to be here? Are you a rebirth of other life forms?"

I don't believe in rebirth, punishments, and blessings taught by some religious sects.

"Justly so, however, you have parents. They had parents. You originate from millennia and generations back, passing on genes that make you the unique being that you are. Have you ever thought about that in terms of your ancestry, your ingesting plant and minerals from the earth that make you the wonderful being that you are? Every iteration of your genes, your participation in the time-space field that you call life binds you to the greater cosmos as well as to your past and future relatives, whether you like them or not. When I made the introduction of myself to you, I introduced myself as a cosmic being. You are one too. Is that so hard to understand?"

> No. Not now. In fact, it makes me feel quite good. It makes me wonder why I have done the stupid and self-destructive things in my life. It also makes me wonder if I could have changed anything, if I could have been wiser.

"Welcome to the galaxy, the universe, TED001."

> If I had made better choices, would the causes have led to better effects?

"No 'Ifs.' The answer to that question is, yes, of course. On many levels of reality you are often and largely where you are because of choices. The universe has billions of choices and consequences occurring simultaneously throughout known time and space. Billions of those thoughts and actions are almost identical in both the choices and consequences.

"You can speculate on whether everything is pre-determined, or determined. Or, if everything determined if it is guided by an intelligent creator, but you will not find the answer in nuclear physics nor even quantum mechanics. Just know that we EBE's, as you call us, recognize in you our own ancestry and holographic relationship to you, and are intervening for no other reason than to deflect you slightly from errors that have been made in the past that have led to unspeakable suffering and pain."

> I just realized that perhaps your mission, or imperative, directive, might be just that, to minimize suffering and pain instead of causing or ending it.

"That's good. The alleviation of pain and suffering should be a global human directive. It is among several directions, the means by which we hope to redirect you from self-destruction, and re-definition of a new consciousness about who and what you are and where you might be someday."

And, obviously, you are not talking about a future heaven, as the major religions profess.

"No, quite unnecessary. Heaven is a figment of Vertical imagination. You have been given a conscious entity you call mind-body on this beautiful blue planet. Locked into the conceptual structure of a Vertical Society, a molecular or holographic one seems remote, especially when I tell you that Terrans must abandon all Vertical institutions--political, religious, social, economic which are cancerous vestiges that will destroy the better nature of humanity, its existence, and the source of its origin. At the center of this threat to your existence and survival is Magical Thinking, dogma based on Magical Thinking and your Vertical assumption that there is no need for rational thinking because 'miracles happen.'"

How is that possible without creating the very things, namely, pain, suffering, and death your directive proposes to avoid or mitigate?

"Sadly, human beings have been told how to make this change numerous times over by visionaries and good men who recognized how Vertical Social structures violate both body and mind and mostly the '*Human Dignity*' that every human being deserves as a creation of a timeless universe. Mohammed and before him Jesus both arrived in your history when tyranny was at its severest Vertical stage. Both attempted to bring something better to their people and to humanity at large. They were both rebels by the standards of the ages in which they appeared."

You might say that in subsequent centuries, the human dignity and rationalization of sight and thought to have been re-discovered in the early fifteenth century has since been lost.

"It has never been lost. It created violent upheavals in western Europe as the Protest of Roman Catholic preachers

119

who wanted to abandon Church hierarchy when they realized by 1500 their beloved Church on the Golden Jubilee of 1500 CE, on the cusp of a new age, was an utterly corrupt and malevolent papacy and papal court.

"That rebellion led to a holographic revision of what it meant to be a Christian. Roman Catholicism was correctly identified by the Protesting priests with the imperialism of the former Roman Empire. Leaders of the Protestant movement appropriately called the corrupt papacy 'Romanism.' This break from the Imperialized Unified (Catholic) Church was an example of holographic thinking. Protestants believed that the papacy and the priesthood both were unnecessary, that every human being could speak directly with God without the necessity of an intervening priest."

It's true. During the sixteenth an seventeenth centuries conflicts abounded as the Roman Church institutionalized the medieval extra-judicial system of the 'Inquisition.'

"After World War II when it was revealed the Vatican had conspired in the holocaust with Nazi (Nationalist-Socialist) Germany, they were forced to reveal records from the late sixteenth through the 20th century. It was learned that the Roman Church had murdered and tortured to death over two-million victims. They kept good records so God would have written documents proving who was unfaithful and deserving their terrible fates. This documentation--as if their 'God' needed printed documents--sealed their complicity in the horrors of Nazi Germany's ethnic cleansing and mass murder made in the name of *lebens raum*—gaining land for the 'superior and pure' Germanic people."

Is that what is happening in other parts of the world today?

"Yes, most notably the Israel and in various branches of the Muslim religion, which for all of the beauty and poetry it created, was born out of the collapse of the Roman empire and the birth of the darkest of the Dark Ages (550-700 CE). Mohammed sought to bring solace and dignity to his own people through a value system he mistakenly thought Judeo-Christian traditions had brought to the near East, even though he believed they had somehow failed. Instead, he inadvertently adopted imperialistic absolutes of the Eastern Roman empire and many of its Vertical traits. Even though he came from a tribal community, a late example of Planar Society, he adopted the imperialism of the Eastern Greek court in Byzantium (modern Istanbul). Most notable is the prostration of men on the floor of a mosque. It was an imperial requirement for those who were in the presence of the Emperor."

It always struck me that Islam discriminates against women when I see Islamic men at prayer in a mosque.

"Islam is not only a by-product of the Roman imperial state, its costumes, separation of women from religious equality and social values, but so is western Christianity in all of its manifestations, including the many sub-sects of Protestantism; namely, in rigid formalism, absolutes of right and wrong, dogma (teachings) intended to brain wash any independent thinking from childhood to adulthood. The current pope explains on the authority of his predecessor Paul II, that women cannot be in the priesthood because Jesus had only male 'apostles.' What a retribalization, returning to the male dominated Vertical Societies of the ancient world without any comprehension of history. History is irrelevant to imperious Vertical authorities. Only symbol and precedent can be accepted into the realm of thought.

"Keepers of Vertical Societies are the most dangerous to molecular or Holographic Societies. As benefactors of that kind of social-economic-religious structure, they will bring great harm to their fellow human beings, employing what you and I can now recognize as sociopaths to carry out their attempts to crush any challenge to the Vertical structure. They are and will be as rapacious as the sub-human sociopaths and teens with no capacity to question authority employed to defend them. This pattern is endlessly repeated in your history. Look at how your corrupted government has created massive secrecy, secret courts with secret agendas. Nothing could be more foreign to freemen and free thinking humans everywhere."

As I well know, but that brings me back to the
issue of Democracy. Can there be a representa-
tive government with a Vertical structure?

"Yes, of course, for a few days or weeks, perhaps even a
month! The concept of a Democracy is antithetical to Verticalized Society. At its best, a Vertical 'democracy is just more
lateralized than a rigid, absolutist state. What Jesus taught
about the human spirit was antithetical to the Vertical Culture of Imperial Rome. He must have realized he was on a
suicide mission."

What about all of the people on the planet now
seeking Democracy?

"Any social group adhering to a Vertical hierarchy cannot expect to make the transition to a true Democracy, least
of all to a Holographic Society, which is what is usually im-
plied by the word 'democracy.' Your defenders of Vertical hierarchy in all political colors, refer to it contemptively as 'So-
cialism.' It is amazing to me that human social structures attempting to depose a tyrannical government, still believe
they can have a traditional, authoritarian-based religion—as
with any of the so-called 'great religions,' and still expect a
democracy to grow out of it.

"None of the Islamic states can achieve any form of Democracy just because they are not able to question any part
of their religious tenants or its representatives, or vote on
their positions. Nor can Islamic faithful have unbiased communications or trade that spans the orb of your planet without being exposed to 'alien' (i.e. non-Muslim) people and
thought, which they must by religious training universally
condemn, even though they are quite accepting of the money
exchanged.

"Democracy is not the birthplace of money or profiteering. Democracy and Vertical Society in all of its manifestations are antithetical, incompatible, and will bring only endless grief if any attempt is made to marry the two. Those
states bound by religious rule and rulers or demagogic absolutist political systems are the most dangerous to the survival
of all life on the planet. I would suggest that if the planet were

destroyed, it would be initiated by an imperialized Vertical religion."

Why do you call those religions authoritarian?

"Two reasons should stand out to you by now. First, any authority derives from a tradition that claims to be divinely dispensed. By definition it is *de facto* unimprovable and at the same time inviolate. You are not allowed to challenge it. Second, the fact that you cannot challenge the divine attribution of religious authority, the latter is the major part of the problem. All paths of exchange--verbal, historical, monetary--are not to be questioned for any reason in a severely verticalized Vertical structure. Authority divinely dispensed can never be questioned and therefore undemocratic and mutually incompatible. The more Vertical a social order, the more severe and uncompromising the understanding of the purpose of religion will be. Religious groups adopting absolutist ideas to confront modern problems are going to be the most dangerous to your legal system you call a 'democracy'"

Therefore, free thinking is a forbidden act, correct?

"It depends on the degree of collective delusion. In the face of modern science any Vertical structure must necessarily be anathema. Do you understand why your current state of scientific inquiry is incompatible with religious authority?"

It's obvious to me. Modern science requires a consensus based on research and testing new hypotheses and conclusions made by other scientists.

"While that is true, there is a more fundamental difference between scientific authority versus religious authority. Scientific inquiry makes a basic assumption that all conclusions, all scientific proofs may be proven wrong or incorrect. No religion can stand up to that. The last thing a religion wants to contend with is someone challenging divinely appointed representatives of magically, two-dimensionally dispensed magical ideas.

"Nothing under the guise of religion can be challenged, whereas scientific inquiry demands that all 'proofs' be proven and re-proven, based on the given assumption that all scientific conclusions are subject to be proven wrong."

> Do you mean even scientific 'principles' on which other scientific proofs are based can be questioned?

"Yes, of course. Without that philosophical position, science would be no different from religions. So many are confused by these incompatibilities and in an attempt to prove their religious delusions create pseudo-science. Religions cannot bear the weight of proven and reproving validity, with what in the scientific community can be called 'evidence.'

"Some of the pseudo-scientific attempts to prove historic events as written and rewritten over thousands of years as being a proof of something have become so utterly absurd that they are challenges to the most basic human logic or reason."

> I know people love Magical Thinking. They believe it will work when modern medicine, science, or fate itself might be redirected and undone. It is part of most of our annual celebrations. Christmas and Easter are pretty important concepts and holidays.

"Both are based on earlier concepts of life, death, and renewal. Delusional, Magical Thinking is a form of mental illness. Given a financial reward, reality becomes blatantly perverted and conflated into fantasies that have little to do with reality, real constants. This situation exists with or without the many-labeled mental illnesses identified by the American Psychiatric Association including schizophrenia, discussed earlier. Rather than approaching schizophrenia as a mental disease, we should look at it as a biologically induced brain/chemistry phenomenon that needs to be approached in a more sympathetic and empathetic way. What a schizophrenic experiences is just another form of delusion as practiced by most non-schizophrenic humans on the planet."

> That is really a little extreme. If all the people in the world who professed belief or faith in a

religion were delusional and mentally ill, how could they have possibly accomplished the great masterpieces they made in art, architecture, music, and poetry? That just does not compute.

"Perhaps you have never heard of the 'mad' genius? Before you object again, hear me out. The issue you raise is partly one of semantics. You can see that mad or mentally ill people do not function well, even if they are not delusional. So, the conflict you feel is that my contraction of the words 'delusional' and 'mental illness' bothers you as you might concur that someone who is delusional but not mentally imbalanced could create great artistic monuments, correct?"

I would like to think that delusional people might create great works of art, yes; but to label anyone identifiable as delusional as also mentally ill seems unfair to millions of good people who profess one religion or another.

"A very reasonable summary of the seemingly radical label I am assigning to people who willfully participate in delusional thinking when they promote myths they know are myths. What I am suggesting to you is actually a remarkable compliment. It is another expression of hope we Galactic Entities have in you to allow, as the ancient Greeks sought to believe about themselves, that you are a rational creature, capable of rational thought on many levels.

"I am not asking you to give up your right-brained thoughts or your humanity. I don't think I should have to give testimonial examples of those people and ideas that are based on human reason like the great musicians of the past or great architects, thinkers, and others searching for answers to the unknown. Most of the famous artists we know from history were not immune from the rational knowledge of their time. Their skills, for example, were based on practice and specialized knowledge. Some like Leonardo da Vinci span both *spectra,* using both his creative and scientific minds to serve his need to do things."

No, I am well enough aware of thousands of examples."

"Delusional thinking is something that masks a reality in another guise that may or may not have any relevance to the reality that gave rise to the delusional association made between the mask and reality. This is very important for you to understand TED. In a very superficial way a symbol might be thought of as a delusion, as it is a 'mask' of the thing, an idea, or concept it is meant to represent."

That makes sense. So why do you call it delusional thinking when it is really symbolic thinking.

"Excellent, now we are getting somewhere. Any beings having the capacity for abstract thought can create a symbol, a shorthand for a condition or system, group, *et cetera*. It is delusional, just the same, because the symbol masks the meaning assigned to it by the maker and can be and is interpreted in many ways. Human sorrow and grief are very real, personal and social traumas are deep wounds in the human psyche that take sometimes years if ever to heal. Loss of a loved one, loss of a life-supporting physiognomy, skin color, of income, or images of constancy and stability all lead to delusional thinking because it seems there are no other answers and answers however abstract, symbolic or self-delusional are thought to be needed in those times."

I am wondering if you really are a superior intellectual being than us humans. I can give you examples that absolutely refute what you are saying: arithmetic, mathematics, words, language are all pure abstractions that mean something and are not delusional, least of all are the people who use these tools of the human mind crazy."

"Crazy is different than mentally ill. Anyway, you bring up a major objection, but it is based on the conflict that humans have with their left and right brains, or between heart and mind, as is often said. Both sides of the human brain (to use a simple example) are in seeming conflict with each other, but that is because both are so deeply interlaced with each other. What can be explained scientifically and rationally sometimes seems irrational and magical at the same time, and likewise the opposite is true. The reason you must ultimately be able to make the distinction of when you are thinking delusionally or magically and when you are thinking rationally, one does not have to explain the other. Both can co-exist, a delusional magical thinker may also be gifted at arithmetic or geometry, physics. Even those who are most rational and realize they cannot answer everything may chose to participate in Magical Thinking for whatever reason."

     I don't understand this vice versa, overlapping
     kinds of thinking.

"Of course you don't. They are intrinsically incompatible. That is the current human flaw. Emerging out of a world that is based on Magical Thinking, magical acts, magical numbers, magical plants and animals, magical words, magical places, and so on, humanity is by definition in a terribly confused and disoriented state.

"As a member of that culture, you are flopping through time like a fish out of water. Confusion promotes a desire for certainty, the emergence of ever-new conflicts between a rational view of reality and a delusional, magical one creates a mental equivalent of Post-Traumatic Stress Disorder."

     I would have to agree. I am feeling a twinge of
     mental confusion, anger, and disbelief just
     having this conversation."

"Quite understandable. Be at peace. I am not trying to upset your mental stability. If you feel that way, unstable at the moment; anger, it is, by definition, <u>not</u> a form of mental illness."

     I don't like the term 'mental illness.' I know I'm
     not crazy. Couldn't we say 'disoriented?'"

"Surely, if you like. Delusional thinking is a process of trying to make the irrational and a-rational cope with the rational. When there are no explanations immediately available, humans create their own explanations, very much like little children do, introducing what may seem absolutely good rational answers and explanation.

"On one of your TV shows a host was interviewing Kindergartners. He asked them if they knew who the president of the United States was. Surprised somewhat that they knew the answer; he then asked them who the vice president was. They replied, 'His wife.' They were participating in delusional thinking based on the known structure of their family life.

"Delusional thinking does not become mental illness until the contradiction with the facts or reality is adopted as an unquestionable truth or fact by a larger community and the absence of that delusion is only unknown as a delusion. If older children or adults adopt the idea that the vice president is now and always will be the wife of the president, then it becomes a form of mental illness. Your beliefs that the United States has a good form of government, has done great things for the world at large, is a form of delusion owing largely to ignorance or an unwillingness to observe evidence to the contrary."

I think I'm understanding.

"Just ask yourself if you have a belief about something that everyone around you also believes? In that case, you might take some comfort in the community of believers. However, if the conflict between a collective idea conflicts more and more with evidence to the contrary, then in order to continue the delusion, someone will step in to enforce the unsupportable community belief at which point a level of oppression occurs. That oppression creates a false delusional world not unlike what is defined as schizophrenia.

"Whole societies over vast geographical areas can reach this kind of impasse between what is real and what is belief and become slaves of their own incapacity to have a healthy mental view of their part of the world. At war with themselves, they burden others with war."

So, if I understand you correctly, you are saying belief is delusion, delusion is mental illness if there is a conflict between what is believed, and what is real. So, why is belief delusion?

"Again, it's a semantic question. You probably believe that gravity is pretty constant, that you are not going to fly off into space if you jump too high. You know if you fall from a ladder, you might get hurt."

Of course I believe that.

"Then don't confuse belief based on rational experience as being identical with belief in a doctrine or dogma (teaching). Because all beliefs are interwoven with the operands of survival, people feel very threatened by challenges to their irrationally and collectively based beliefs. This threat is compounded by their knowledge of great art, poetry, music, and literature based on their religious and cultural traditions, which for them are cultural proofs of beliefs."

I think that if someone believes something, it makes it true for that person and his community of believers."

"That may be very generous of you, but to challenge anything, great or small, will generate terror in the minds of many people, who, under a false or even the most minimal threat to their personal or group adopted delusion, can be led to believe their very lives and culture are threatened with extinction."

My mom used to think that. She said we had to go to church every Sunday because if we didn't Christianity would disappear and so would America."

"You know what I am saying, sociopaths who blow up themselves and anyone nearby, kill school children, drop bombs on homes, machine gun unarmed children and adults from helicopters, or plan a nuclear death for the entire world do nothing for the causes they claim. Because you declare faith in this or that concept or belief, go to a mosque, synagogue, or church, or sing the national anthem, bow and repeat programmed prayers, do you think anything will change for the better or would give you the right to bring endless suffering, death and pain to others? These acts are a mockery of anything that could be called divine, godly, or humane. Who then is delusional?"

How does that compare to a Holographic Society?

"You must understand that a Vertical Society cannot exist with endless variables challenging every level of interaction. You must first learn how to effectively raise a child.

Those first critical hours after birth the infant must be accompanied by contact between the newborn and the mother or surrogate parent. This is the follow-up to prenatal care once a pregnancy occurs in the form of the mother avoiding toxins in alcohol, drugs, cigarettes, and allergenic foods and giving as much visual and auditory stimulation to the child. Once the mother and child are in their home, the mother and child must engage in right-brain to right-brain communication as a singularly conscious effort as the social and intellectual ground work for the development of the child in its first three years of life.

"It must be consistent and with knowledge. Intimacy is a human's greatest need throughout life, but especially in those first hours, months, and years of life. The needs of the child and eventually of every adult, is a community."

That seems like a practical possibility. Why isn't that systematically done since the effects of that kind of mother-child interaction are now well understood?

"You are asking me? All living things are dependent upon community. Isn't that how we started out? You want to become part of the greater universe, the galactic community, the community of God, as you call it in many iterations. Good. You are asking for information. Let's talk about that.

LOG XIV

THE PAN DISSEMINATION OF KNOWLEDGE AND IDEAS

"Have you noticed how much people enjoy devices like the Internet and Twitter?"

Who doesn't? When the first computers came out, I realized that there could be no greater freedom of thought than what could be shared by millions of people on their own personal computers. In fact, I thought that it would help democratize the world, especially when the Internet became part of every computer--and it has, as we see all over the world. People could learn about each other instantly and share their knowledge and histories.

"Yes, and just for that reason I asked such an innocuous question. Information, and the use and interrelationships of information is knowledge. By giving access to billions of bits of information, people can live and work in a more informed environment, unless suppressed."

What you are leading up to is pretty obvious. Suppression of information is essential to the survival of the Vertically structured state, right?

"IGNORANCE is the life-blood of Vertical Societies, especially if it can be assured among masses of the population."

You mean like the control of the media in China.

"China! In every Vertical Society information is limited to the boundaries of tolerance. Your media in the U.S. is a prime example. All of your radio stations are controlled by corporate entities, almost all radio stations in the U.S. by the Clear Channel corporation. There are a few independent stations, and a larger number of semi-controlled stations under the heading of Public Broadcasting, but these are constantly under threat of having any and all financial resources cut by the Federal government, especially by the right wing controllers and protectors of your imperious Vertical Society.

"Republicans and some Southern Democrats have consistently sought to profitize all functions of government by privatizing them. They know that every 'contractor' for the government is at the deep feeding trough of the ignorant American taxpayer. Your television stations are the same. You are not going to hear or see anything broadcast by so-called independent media that is not going to be controlled by both government and as most invested entities in a Vertical Society."

Conservatives,' as they call themselves, think the media are too liberal and liberals, as they are called by conservatives, think they are too conservative.

"TED, these are disguised labels since both extremes never question the efficacy or inherently autocratic hierarchy of a Vertical culture. Both support an innately authoritarian and ultimately totalitarian system."

Yet, you have to admit there is still a great deal of freedom of thought or no achievements would be made, no progress.

"I agree. Having flushing toilets and toilet paper is real progress. What in heaven's name is 'progress' unless fundamental psychological and social changes have been made? If you follow any product or idea to its end, its point of obsolescence, you will find that a small group benefitted by the exchange of money and the general population is no better off."

Well, I'm not sure about toilet paper.

"O.K., I've been talking to you long enough to know that there is a ton of information about to spill out that will represent the utter destruction of information and knowledge in a Vertical Society.

"As we just observed, Vertical Societies are inherently opposed to dissemination of information in order to maintain the artifice of hierarchic Verticality. At various times in human history, knowledge is considered a priestly privilege. Sacred knowledge cannot be made available to the masses.

Magicians and wise men do not tell their secrets. Knowledge and information are always held close to throne and altar, both located at the apex of the Vertical Society. Vertical Societies require secret knowledge so that people who control can do so with the acquiescence and even the celebration of the majority population."

It disgusts me that there are so many people who make a mockery of intelligence and knowledge, like bikers and blue collar workers in general. They see it as quite useless unless it can be translated into something they can use, play with, drink, frighten enemies, or put in their bank.

"I'm glad you mention 'frightening enemies.' But why single out bikers? The arms and war industries of the Terran world depend on such information to be held as a secret as long as possible to give them an edge over their enemies, or long enough to profit from their manufacture before becoming obsolete; then, the 'obsoletes' are sold to their enemies. Bikers, my friend, are no different than the uninformed or elderly ladies at church who do the same thing. For them, God is in control and that's all anyone needs to know."

For my parents and most, I think, their belief and faith were the most honorable and important words in their lives. These qualities applied not only to their church but to their country and their values.

"Listen to me, 'Belief' and 'Faith' are code words for the requirement of domination and control by others. They deny the necessity or reality of tested and confirmed evidence and statistical probability. Real, legitimate information, tested proof is a fuse that sparks a fire that lights up, a flame that burns for centuries. I want to propose to you our way of approaching information and knowledge."

I can't wait.

"You will recall that I surprised you when I suggested a moneyless exchange system, and surprised you even more when I suggested that everything should be available to virtually everyone if so desired."

Yes, I was a little surprised, and I still hope you are going to explain it further, because I still don't see how it could work, even if there were no greed, covetousness, gluttony, self-indulgence and the like.

"We will get to those issues in due time. Meanwhile consider the possibility that all information is accessible at all times by everyone, for anyone interested."

That definitely wouldn't work. People take pride in their literature, their research, their achievements, their products and should be rewarded for making their contributions to society. What do you do about copyrights and intellectual property?

"And lawyers? In a stage three Holographic Society a lawyer is as useful as a priest or magician. With the technology you already have, you could credit everyone for his or her invention, work of art, intellectual property, whatever contribution they wish to make. With that technology, you can also record all related thoughts and ideas, building evidence and concepts into three-dimensional diagrammatic trees of information. As soon as someone has an opinion or thought, they can deposit it on an intelligent interactive database. Your 'Cloud' may be a prefatorial example. If it is identical to someone else's, it can be shown either to be derivative or independent of anything that has appeared earlier, show if it is simultaneity of thought, or entirely original.

"Billions of designs, thoughts, phrases, books, research articles, can be deposited as fast as your storage system will permit. You look upon the National Security Agency collecting billions of numbers and conversations every day as a 'probable' intrusion on your privacy. In a Holographic Society you can choose your level of participation and reap the benefits."

If there is no money, then what is the benefit?

"The benefit is that information is constantly being refreshed, updated, clarified, or reclaimed sometimes long after, even centuries, of being ignored. The latter are intrinsic benefits. As for an equivalent to money, everyone has a basic value intrinsic to their very being, and by that I do not mean the minerals that might be left behind after one is cremated."

I'm glad to hear that, because our bodies are supposed to be worth about $1.75.

"Much more. As a member of the cosmos, you are valued as a living entity. You have a guarantee from the moment of conception until your death that you will always have a place to reside, food to eat, transportation, any tools and material things you may need for day-to-day living, and complete medical coverage. When Jefferson wrote that every citizen of the world has a right 'to life, liberty, and the pursuit of happiness,' he was declaring a universal truth, even though he personally held other humans in bondage."

I always thought that the first right 'the right to life' should be a right to health and medicine as needed, otherwise the right to liberty and the pursuit of happiness are rarely possible if you are in ill health, even if you have a simple but painful dental problem. Not only that, it seems that every Congressman and Senator has managed to give him/herself a medical insurance plan better than any citizen they supposedly represent.

"Right. The inequities of a Vertical Society are not only grossly unfair, but cost people their lives for no other reason than they do not have access to food, shelter, or medical care because they are not truly valued as human beings and because they are poor and relocated to the lower or underclasses."

The Vertical tiers or levels of economic classes are discussed all the time. It seems a natural result of classifying those on different levels of income, on which taxes are proportional. Some professions which are more important than others receive proportionate incomes.

"With investigation you will discover nothing is really proportionate. In a moneyless, Holographic Society, there is no need to pursue a profession because of the money it will bring over a short or long period. Since we live an average of

300 to 500+ years longer than Terrans, you can see why we need to value everyone equally and provide the basic subsistences because each of us share the view that we are intrinsically valuable and not because we have climbed to positions on a Vertical ladder, because they are assumed to be inherently more valuable. Nobody needs a well-paid Adolf Hitler, or any sociopath because they offer solace to the psychologically and financially distressed. Nobody should go without because others are what you call 'successful.'"

But I'm troubled by this idea of a no money economy. What would women do if they could not shop?

"It's called 'shopping' only because it is search for the best price, but what women are really doing is something they have done for millennia."

I can't imagine what that could be. I am bored by shopping. Men know what they want. They go into a store, find it or not. If they find it, that's it. They buy it. So what have women been doing for millennia?

"Women are looking for the best for themselves and their families. Their looking for the best root vegetables, leaf vegetables, berries, fruit; they are caring for their families as an unconscious survival mechanism dating back to the most primitive times of Planar Society. Your monetary systems not only makes them look foolish, but become foolish thinking that what they are 'shopping' for will bring them admiration and envy that they should have so much credit or money allowing them to purchase all the things they do. Such values are worthy only of a nubile, pubescent teen."

So what does this have to do with information?

"Everything! In a Vertical Society everything is about ownership, possession, power, symbols of power, symbols of authority, and often times a symbol of contempt for anyone who does not have equal or greater controlling or consumptive power. Just as the ancients and later the monumental religious organizations compiled libraries of what was thought to be secret information, and proofs of claims of things divine. It was important to keep the masses of the

136

population ignorant of their own languages, writing, inter-preting, and reciting known written compilations they deemed as sacred.

"If you are not initiated into the sacred rites of 'know-ing' then you could not see, touch, or hear divine words or things. With the birth of writing, stories soon emerged that are both fairy tales of fantastic images and ideas along with pieces of entirely credible information. Private museums, private libraries, presidential libraries are really symbols of wealth and power having little to do with knowledge or crea-tive thought."

Didn't Alexander the Great establish the first library in the city named after him, Alexan-dria?

"Undoubtedly not the first! The Egyptians compiled them first. Libraries were known throughout the Greek speaking world, most after the model of Alexander's library. They were known in Athens, Nicosia, Pergamon, and else-where, but these came long after Alexander raided all of the sacred temple libraries of Egypt to unhinge Egyptian reli-gion, rights of ownership, and the general political system by putting all records in one place."

That was a good way of controlling the elites.

"Napoleon, in his contempt for Roman Catholicism and following Alexander's example, did the same with the mo-nastic libraries of Italy after conquering the Italian penin-sula, putting their documents in public archives. If you can gain control of documents of ownership, knowledge, sacred information, a Vertical Society loses all of its reference ma-terial on which its Vertical structure is built."

From this conclusion, I would guess that to preserve a social order, you need to steal all of the old history and build a new one.

"It's not quite that easy, but you've got the general idea. If you intend to marry a conquered society with a new one, the conqueror must win over the population of the masses."

How can you do that with all the information sequestered?

"You are assuming the conquered population immediately forgets their past, their relationships, and their ceremonies. That just does not happen. How do you think the Roman Catholic Church was so astute at converting millions not only to a new religion, but convincing the conquered peoples to learn the languages of the conquering armies? To answer my own question, they merge the doctrine and ceremonies of each local social group with those of the Roman Church, so that the break appears less severe. This is largely the difference between the Protestant European method of absolute military conquest in the form of a Vertical tyranny over the native peoples of North America, in contrast to the subjugation of Central and South American cultures by the Roman church."

> You mean the protestant Americans were worse? What about Alexander VI's Bull of 1493 that demanded the natives of the Americas be given the choice of accepting the authority of the Pope or they would be killed. That isn't what happened with the Peruvian Incas. They were annihilated, too, weren't they?

"No one knows for sure. Maybe the Vatican librarians could tell you, certainly not all Incans. The Spanish captured the Inca chief then ordered him to bring all the gold to one place in order to save his life. He did so, and was then summarily executed. Coming from a rigidly axial Vertical Society, the Spanish conquistadores over what is now modern Peru were monstrously cruel, no doubt after the model of the medieval crusades and the papal dictum of 1493 you mentioned. To further humiliate the Incas and the Aztecs and natives of the Yucatan, the Roman Church built cathedrals directly over the most sacred sites of the original native population."

> So, if information is hidden, sequestered, and even destroyed, isn't there some way to resist the conquerors?

"If your means of social organization is uprooted and your leaders slain, imprisoned, or threatened with the option of death or conversion to the new structure, you are left with only the outer garments of the former order such as styles of clothing, food, dance, and popular magic. In some cases, corrupted versions of former societal structures are preserved in social memory, but not as part the new structure except in those instances where the conquering intellectuals can tolerably integrate the new order with the past."

Our society is so complex I would think there is not much point in these methods of conquest. What would happen to ownership in a moneyless society? Forget about real estate, private property. What about ownership of patents and copyrights? These are the real important things in a modern industrial society.

"Copyrights and patents are important only to a profit-based Vertical Society. In a Vertical Society they are only important for control of money. You have a tendency to think that such 'rights' and 'patents' are meant to protect inventors, authors, artists."

Yes, I've copyrighted everything I have written, most of it unpublished. I don't want somebody stealing my ideas and intellectual property and making a giant profit off of it at my expense. I would even guess that the widest, deepest, most far-reaching kind of theft is that of intellectual property. There are lawyers who make a living, defending inventors, writers, film makers, and artists.

"You know the thieving nature of your Vertical Society well. On occasion they defend a writer, artist, or inventor and doing something good, but more often they are defending a corporation which is neutral to good and bad, concerned as they are in a Vertical Society for profit. Because corporations are Vertical Societies within a Vertical Society, they can afford to carry out lawsuits whereas a creative person rarely has the capital to defend him- or herself. Unscrupulous corporations hire lawyers to do the work of soldiers; namely, to destroy any opposition to their intentions to make a profit.

"For example, a famous 'mining' company invented a gene for corn, which when eaten by a corn beetle, would kill the pesty insect. Great for food protection, until a farmer next to a farm where the beetle killing corn was planted found that when he harvested his crop he had no beetles even though he did not have his crop sewn with the same beetle-killing seeds. The mining company then sued the farmer for his profits as the pollen from the newly inseminated plants had blown to his farm. The farmer did nothing but enjoy what he thought was a nice summer breeze, paying dearly for a little wind, through no fault of his own."

I know of other examples too. It seems that the money-based Vertical Society is insidious in its far-reaching implications for all of our lives. Some companies have claims for possessing people's own genes and DNA!

"It is not only insidious, but genocidal. On every level of this hierarchy exists a basic threat to life and the common good. For example, Finland, Sweden, and Denmark are 'social democracies' where individual health is given a priority. These countries are rated as having the best living standards, the best feelings about happiness and life, and the finest and highest rated educational systems."

Those are still Vertical Societies that use money. So, what is different than the U.S. which has the greatest wealth?

"These three countries are all much smaller than the U.S. They have vastly smaller military and secret organizations of government; they pay more taxes than U.S. citizens, but not much more and have national health records that put the U.S. to shame. It is hard to be rated 68th in infant mortality in the world to say nothing of the industrial world, but that is where the U.S. standard lies. It is a popular American claim that they have the best medical system in the world, but it is only a measure of your collective ignorance and by best you mean for those patients who have access to the finest medical institutions because of no other reason than their financial wealth. More people die of starvation, of the lack of minimal health care, obesity, cancer, heart disease in the United States than in many third world countries."

So why is that discrepancy?

"Americans are among the least knowledgeable in the industrial world. You have representatives of these same people who are easily convinced of false assumptions, just like the one I just gave, that the U.S. has the best medical care in the world. It is another delusion, but an induced fear throughout the country where there is a great disdain for education, the cowboy west, for example, and a bugaboo fear of Communism. Social democracy as found in Denmark, Sweden, Norway, and Finland is seen by U.S. citizens as another as a form of Communism, totalitarian style, especially among uninformed mid-westerners, Bible Belt, and macho-based segments of your population. Since the two are simplistically equated, any form of assistance to the poor or unfortunate is considered leaning toward Communism, or leaning too far 'left.' It is the sociopathic side of Vertical Society.

"If so accused, the simple are frightened and do not have the intellectual or educational tools to differentiate the two. They hold this fear even though they are the ones most in need of good health and well-being provided by a government concerned with the common good."

Information, then, can be equated with well-being, makes sense.

"It runs still deeper. You rely too heavily on your popular images, your TV news, Internet videos. Your libraries are closing and any new ones being built are designed in such a way that they can be sold at some time in the future as office buildings or restaurants. You have another undeveloped part of your mind/brain. You call it intuition. Both women and men have it, although because women's left and right frontal lobes are more connected than in males, it appears they have better information."

You have 'Psychics' who pretend or do communicate on other dimensions only predicted by mathematical models into the eleven mathematically projected levels of reality.

"Consider this. If you can know what another person is thinking before that person verbalizes it and do so consistently, you are communicating telepathically. If you can do this at virtually any distance, what does that say about secrecy and honesty? You Terrans struggle with honesty all of the time, not only because you cannot understand another person's thoughts, but because you do not know yourself. Often, when you do perceive something profoundly real you turn it into an external magical experience, a divine inspiration event, so confused you are about the sciences of telepathic communication."

> That must mean, pan-dissemination of knowledge may be going on throughout the galaxy or universe. Is that what you are saying? I would like to think that is possible, but it brings me back to ownership, copyrights, trademarks, all of those things that supposedly protect original thinking.

"TED, we have already discussed that. All those needs for possession are products of Vertical needs for control and for profit-based, money economies. I can attest there is nothing new in the universe. The veritable *Encyclopedia Galactica* is simply a gigantic Internet. With your Internet, you are at least one billionth of the way there."

> So, how do you become an architect? Who do you build for if there is such a thing as an architect? What do your buildings look like? Some of the most spectacular buildings humans have ever created and the art created for and as part of them, remain as images of awe and wonder, aesthetic appreciation long after the motivations for building them has long disappeared. Do you have anything like that?

"Yes, beauty is so much a part of the universal mind and nature, as beautiful as a rose flower blooming. Humans are that way too. You are harmonically organized in your brain and proportions, an exceptional product the fullness and abundance of life in the universe.

"Realize, please, every solar system demonstrates an abundance of life, creating and recreating itself forever. Your own planet has offered you an example of what you might find anywhere in the billions of solar systems, just in this galaxy of which you and I are a part.

"Rejoice in the prospect that your children and their families may visit the vast oceans of space and time, the energy, the colors, the sounds so spectacular that your terrestrial history will seem so tragic and senseless in the consequences of ill-conceived, misinterpretations of what a human mind and life could be. Isn't that a promise?"

Yes, I think so. I think about these things a lot. I know millions of others also think about the things produced just in their creative imaginations, even if they do not become physical realities. I would like to communicate telepathically, but there must be some rules, even if you can do it and most of us can't. It seems like it would be infinitely faster than my present methods of thinking, whatever they are, electro-chemical I guess.

Aren't you embarrassed most of the time, though, I mean thinking as often as we do of very private, intimate or crazy things? To say nothing of copyrights and patents, what about 'invasions of privacy?'

LOG XV

VERTICAL VS. HOLOGRAPHIC
ARCHITECTURE

X, I am so disoriented by so many things you
are telling me, that I keep coming back to primary questions, questions I have been asking
myself since this dialogue began.

"Understandable and I am quite aware of your back-
ground thoughts. They are quite legitimate questions to ask.
The kinds of environments we create for yourselves mirror
the socio-religious-political environments in which humans
live; therefore, it is one of the first questions we would expect
you to ask of a stranger. In Horizontal and Vertical Societies
you build environments as shelter to protect your physical
well-being as well as for your social well-being."

You mean you do not need to protect yourself?

"Yes, but in ways that are so far-removed from your
Vertical Societies that you would probably have a hard time
recognizing the what, where and why of our so-called shelters would look like or be. Let's just look at Vertical Society
architecture and environmental planning as far as the latter
goes."

I know. You are going to point to the pyramids
of Egypt, of Central America, China, and
mound builders all over the globe.

"I have already brought up the pyramids in various
places, obvious metaphors of Vertical Societies with top-
down social, political, and religious conceptual structures. I
have also mentioned the phallic nature of modern high rise
buildings as metaphors of male ownership of property and
subordinated renters, in a top-down hierarchy. Unfortunately, these observations only go so far to describe the Verticality of the hierarchy of a money-based society. Most
buildings in the 20th and 21st centuries adhere to a slave/
master relationship. Those that do not are usually public
benefit buildings such as museums, concert centers, and
sports."

Once again, I am already wondering how you
can say something like that, but go on.

"TED, have you ever looked at a computer 'mother
board' or even a simple circuit board with its square and rectangular chips and running streets of pathways tying the cir-
cuits together?"

http://media.photobucket.com/user/sportto-
night/media/Chipset_Notebook.jpg.html?

Yes, even the insides of the CPU's, CMOS, and
RAM chips look like that, sort of like Piet Mondrian's painting.

"So you are acquainted with abbreviations of their technical names, but also their similarity to street and building-
like patterns, much like the Dutch painter Mondrian's
Broadway Boogie Woogie?"

https://www.moma.org/collection/works/78682

Yeah, little did Mondrian know his painting
would become so relevant to later 20th century
technology.

"When architectural firms like Skidmore Owings and
Merrill created rectangular boxes of steel and glass, the inte-
riors are similarly planned to maximize the output of the humans working inside for one or more corporations. These
buildings are carefully engineered not only to stand up under
great pressures and even movements of wind and earth, but
to maximize the productivity of the people inside.

https://en.wikipedia.org/wiki/Skidmore,_Ow-
ings_%26_Merrill

"These buildings are like Central Processing Units
(CPU's) but most importantly, they are People Processing
Units (PPU's), or "Towers of Power." Your modern, 'sky-
scraper' buildings segregate people on the outside from those
inside by making the activities of those inside invisible. Glass
walls not only keep out or minimize sunlight, but make those
inside voyeurs of those on the outside and themselves
framed in, depersonalized, processing units. Some of these
buildings do look like phalluses, others like robots, but al-

most all are forms of rigid prisons of people working for minimal wages or for financial returns that on average are so dis-
proportionately small."

> This sounds something like Marshall McLu-
> han's *'the medium is the message.'* Vertical So-
> cieties build Vertical buildings as fancy sweat-
> shops, is that what you're saying? Seems kind
> of simple.

"In part, yes, but not the most important thing. Like so
many of your sports, buildings are gravity defying. The fact
that they rise so high becomes an act of defying gravity, but
such buildings would be utterly useless without elevators. Elevators defy gravity. They use up enormous amounts of energy to make this levitation possible. Then, once you are at
an 'observation deck' near the top of the building you can
look down in awe at the scene below, just as Mondrian was
doing when he came to New York city the first time and drew
the analogy of a popular music form of the time with the rec-
tilinearity and busy traffic on the streets below."

> Absolutely! I've often wondered who owned
> most of the high rises in the world and what
> their personal psychological view of them-
> selves was.

> "I suppose everyone would like to know that."
> So, X, if someone like Antoni Gaudì, Robert
> Buckminster-Fuller, or more recent architects
> like Koolhaas, Gehry, or Hadid, would you con-
> sider them moving toward a holographic archi-
> tecture?

"Somewhat. The modern architect lives in a world
where alternative sources of energy are being explored in totally unique ways. Nonetheless, high rises as PPU's keep being built and will be as long as Terrans still hang onto Vertical culture, a multiplicity of Verticalities, vying with other
Verticalities define its architecture. In most situations, especially in public governmental buildings with their domes, ob-
elisks, and pyramidal caps, the expression of "power over" is

entirely sexual. You can see this exposed phallicism everywhere. Towers of Power are simply expressions of sexual power.

https://www.google.com/search?q=City%20H all,%20Los%20Ange-les&tbm=isch&ufsmps=1&gws_rd=cr&c=5441

"In a Holographic Society, you would probably have a hard time finding a building anywhere on a holographic planet. What is the need for high-rise buildings if you have the capability to easily raise any weight with the least amount of energy and no need architectural monuments to demonstrate wealth and power? No need to destroy the land in order to build structures."

Are you saying an advanced civilization would not have cities or they would be deep in the ocean or underground? Neither of those seem very appealing to me. Underground or underwater cities would mean going back to a troglodytic or worse, a bathyspheric type of living. You know, '*We All Live in a Yellow Submarine.*'

"You left out space ships. You can't get away from the Beatles. It's a rather dirty green, I'd say. A submarine is a spaceship, right?"

Why do you say the structures of a Holographic Society would be invisible? Is it true that your cities are under water or underground?

"Yes, and no. But you are still thinking in terms of cities and city-based civilization oriented around a sacred Place. You have already seen our so-called cities."

I have?

"Every GE group has its own forms of transportation environments. Some are disc-like, others like cigars, some like walnuts. In as much as intergalactic transport vehicles (IGTV's) they must be able to sustain life very much as you air craft and space vehicles. As each planetary people solve the problem of defying gravity liberating themselves from

147

the ownership and expense of harvesting and redirecting natural resources. For us, it is no longer necessary to annihilate whole forests, mountains, lakes, and natural landscapes to sustain the Vertical necessity of a sacred Place.

"Once you solve the anti-gravitational energy problem, you are no longer confined to Place. Places cease to become notable, historically important, and least of all sacred. All of your wars over Place are senseless claims that senselessly cost millions of lives. You claim to consider human life sacred, but never hesitate at sending sons and daughters into the hell of mass murder over delusions about the importance of domination over Place."

So, in Star Trek, when they come upon Klingon territorial boundaries in space are the writers of that screenplay are transferring Vertical concepts to the vastness of space?

"There seem to be no boundaries to your preference for stories and images based on delusions, Hollywood delusions at that. Do you not know you have no boundaries on your oceans? The oceans are analogous to solar and galactic space. No one owns any part of it. Yes, some Terran nation states claim a 12 mile extension into the ocean of their national boundaries, some as much as 100 miles, but you think instead in terms of the fantasy of Star Trek."

I guess I like our delusions and fantasies.

"Indeed, you do. Unfortunately, you cannot tell one from the other. That is because the concept of Vertical order is deeply embedded in your thought processes."

One of our pet ideas, illusions, or delusions we all seem to share, at least in the U.S., is the idea that '*a man's home is his castle.*' We like to create environments that satisfy us. Most of us want our homes to be safe places to do the ordinary things of human life. We often want that home to be near work, near access to utilities, near schools for our children.

We want that home to be a kept environment, a garden of sorts, if only a green grass lawn and a few trees. We want it to be a place where friends and family can come and visit, share meals on special days and we like to decorate our home's inner and outer spaces with some aesthetic sense that becomes an expression of our lives as couples and as parents. We prefer to live in locations that are either aesthetically pleasing, near friends and family, or are communities of status and safety.

Likewise, the variations on the community environment are important to us as the larger community represents much the same as our individual living spaces. We consider high-rise living in a bee-hive environment less than satisfactory and know that in places where governments have attempted to house large numbers of people in housing projects, the results are not happiness but social chaos.

"You speak truthfully TED001, however long-windedly. If you can, attempt to parse out the parts of your comments that arise from the Vertical Society that gave rise to these ideas. After you strip the delusions and fantasies from the realities, fill in the blank spaces where you have left out large portions of your reality, which has many shortcomings and benefits, then you will know a little better what you really have and what is important to you."

Well, right away, I think those things I mentioned would not be possible on a space-ship, even a cigar-shape as has supposedly observed a mile in diameter and 20 to 25 miles in length out near Jupiter and flying toward earth. That is a pretty big ship.

Even so, I doubt you are going to find nice houses with gardens and fences in that kind of ship. Even more likely, you are not going to find privacy and a place to withdraw from the crowd. We humans like intimacy in sexual relationships but also in friendships and quiet moments with our own thoughts.

"Do not dismiss us. Being liberated from gravity, from the sacredness of Place, the Vertical Society and all that it implies, does represent a major intellectual and psychological transition. If suddenly imposed on Terrans, much of the race would wither and die as occurred to hundreds of thousands of Native Americans throughout the Americas with the arrival of Verticalized Europeans. No artillery, musket, bayonet or rifle, were necessary. The same happened among the islanders of the south Pacific. Terrans rightly have just as great a fear from the effects of culture shock as from foreign invasion."

So, X, you agree that we are close to our environment, that we would have a hard time adjusting to a Holographic Society, even though we seem to be moving in that direction.

"Absolutely! That is the reason we are here, to guide you through that inevitable transition. No one is bringing it upon you but yourselves. Vertical Society is unsustainable and has so many built-in negative or self-destructive assumptions that it creates a universal imbalance not only on planet earth but among the star systems of the galaxy. "

That is pretty far-reaching, how our little planet and our actions could have such a mega-historical effect.

"They do. You are part of a vast hologram. Everything is related to everything else. There are no hierarchies, there are no higher and lower values, upper and lower statuses or positions, there are no Sacred Places, no places called heaven, there are no saints, gods or deities. The universe is your place. You and all life are cosmic beings made of the same stuff.

"The more humans hold onto the singularities of their Vertical-based assumptions and beliefs, the worse their lives and survivability becomes. Once the violence, intransigence, foolishness, transgressions of people against people, people against the environment, and the inequities of the Vertical Society are recognized, the sooner such things as 'defense,' armies and navies, nuclear weapons, corporations, churches, charitable societies, jails and prisons will be seen as obsolete, dangerous, and in the end, useless."

Does that mean there is no architecture to a Holographic Society at all?

"No, not really. It just means only the wholesome and real based on evidence, can become acceptable as sustaining."

That sounds less than believable. So, what is 'wholesome and real?' Who enforces the acceptable and sustaining?

"Until you can transcend your axial thinking, it doesn't matter. It is another subject more understandable at a later time. In the meantime, we need to prioritize your stepwise withdrawal from the Vertical System that seems so critical to your survival and integrate into the Holographic Society you are already stepping into."

Yeah, I wouldn't want to pull the rug out too soon.

"I am not promoting a revolution. A revolution is already in process. You call it evolution, but it's not that slow. Perhaps the most notable is the global Internet"

Cool.

"About as cool as a habanero."

Most important, what do you think is our greatest danger X? You have pretty well said we are the greatest danger to ourselves and the environment. I think it will be easier to change something technological than the smallest part of human nature.

So, let's start there. What technological change do we need to make first to help insure the survival of humans and this planet?

"That's easy. The ancient Greeks and before them the earlier Minoans devised several tales about human trespassing upon the rights and capabilities of the 'gods.' Such trespasses were considered *hubris*, a crossing of boundaries between humans and the gods humans were not meant to cross. An act of *hubris* was punishable by death.

"Among many similar stories was the story of Icarus, the son of the famous architect of the Palace at Knossos, Crete, called Daedalus. Icarus, who was as ingenious as his father, full of himself, and wanting to fly, constructed what you would call today a hang-glider made of wooden ribs, string, and eagle feathers, the latter held together with beeswax. He successfully took off, soon flying high above the palace, then over the island of Crete and the Aegean Sea. In his hubris, he sailed so high that the sun melted the beeswax. One by one feathers melted off and Icarus plunged to his death in the sea.

"An equally poignant act of hubris was the discovery of fire by Prometheus. Fire, like flight, belonged only to the gods and for his punishment he was chained to a rock where birds fed on his body until in utter agony Prometheus also received his reward for attempting to do something only the gods were allowed to possess."

I understand why you bring up these stories. You want to show me that the most important act for all people in a Vertical Society is obedience to higher authority. But what is the technological connection? We <u>should</u> not try to fly?

"At last you are beginning to read me better, but no. While you are correct that the virtue of obedience as one of the exalted virtues of Vertical Societies, that is not the main reason I mention these stories to you.

"In each act of hubris humans are in a no-win situation. Once fire is captured and used, all kinds of consequences arise from its use from baking bread to burning whole villages and cities. Technological discovery is always a blessing and a curse.

"Even though Icarus met a tragic end, all humans have at one point or another envied the floating birds in the air, free, it would seem, of gravity. Even to wish for flight was an act of hubris all humans in one manner or another wish or dream they could achieve as your civilization realized in the last century."

Unfortunately, almost immediately, flight was used at the beginning of WW-II to commit mass murder by dropping bombs, strafing and killing on a scale never before possible. Tested first on the little town of Guernica.

Obviously, flight is a blessing and a curse. Ancient Greek mythologists contrived their stories as metaphors for the limitations of humans to create technologies for which they can foresee the consequences. So, before we go into space or pride ourselves in the nuclear power of the atom, we might attempt to conceive the consequences. Am I right this time, X?

"Precisely, but is it done? Are measures taken to safeguard the populations near and far from failures of nuclear power plants, or storing deadly residual radioactive materials such as Cesium, Iodine, Strontium, and Plutonium, to mention just a few by-products that remain deadly to most animal life for millions and in some cases billions of years? The planners and builders of nuclear power plants (NPP's) design for one to withstand a minor earthquake, or a passenger jet crashing into the building. But what do they do with nuclear "waste?" It is not really "waste," but a new and powerful thing like trying to bury a giant living animal, the legendary Godzilla. When they realize they must transport that "waste" by train and truckload to be secretly stored in locations where it is thought there would be minimal risk of being stolen or affecting human water supplies, they are gambling. But, you must ask, gambling for the next tens of thousands of years? Is that not hubris?"

Seems like it to me.

"They also design these NPP's to last an estimated 20 years, but rarely are they shut down after their life-expectancy has passed. Even if they do shut them down, the danger of these installations will last for millions of years. How long can the designers expect to keep such radioactive materials free from over-heating, or keep pumps running to cool radioactive locations. Tubing and pipes cooling water passes through and environments around nuclear plants deteriorate?

"You already know too well the constant threat of global annihilation by nuclear war and yet humans cannot find a solution to global conflict or war profiteering. Residues of current and former battle fields where every rifle shell, machine gun bullet, artillery shell and most bombs are veneered with depleted uranium, which take thousands of years to deteriorate to safe levels."

Why do they use depleted uranium?

"Because it is a hard material that often penetrates whatever it hits. Iraqi and Afghan farmers will be tilling soil spread with radioactive materials that will last a billion years. How long do you think human civilization will last in its present conformities and structures? What happens to people exposed to these radiation levels by farming or eating contaminated animals and plants that you and the animals eat? The answer is in the innumerable deformities of children being born in these war zones and the explosions of cancers. Your cancer rates are becoming a plague in the northern hemisphere.

"I ask you, is it any wonder that humans are constantly preoccupied with death? Perhaps by imaging it in death's heads, crosses, ceremonies celebrating the dead, or days of the dead, the unconscious belief is that they own it and therefore it cannot touch them by surprise, a kind of delusional immunization."

I didn't realize such horrific things were happening.

"How could you? None of your news media would dare show the consequences of your wars for profit, or death by nuclear fallout. They are not going to realistically look at the constancy of war hardware or affected plants and animals including humans to suffered from self-destructive evidence.

"In a Vertical Society, all features of that society devolve into control groups. At your present state, control groups are major owners of property and one percent of the one percent who control 94% of the wealth of the entire economy of the U.S. The majority of this 1% controls all of the sources of energy, but also secret information about those things they cannot control."

That's not possible because there are public oversight commissions.

"Ask yourself, who appoints the commissioners? These are the people who have massive investments in the current state of energy resources and equally massive financial returns because they control the public utility commissions, radio and television news."

You are saying that everything protecting the public is fraudulent.

"I am saying that Vertical social structures require corruption and favoritism as the hierarchy is fixed on financial returns. You call this upward flow of human energy and wealth 'success.' In most cases it is a structured theft. When the experiments in free (zero-point) energy by Tesla were presented to J.P. Morgan, his response was *'If I can't put a meter on it, I don't want it.'* Now you have a financial elite who have invested heavily in nuclear power plants, 104 in your country alone. Two have been shut down recently and others are being recognized as too dangerous to relicense.

"Japan's Fukushima disaster should be a lesson in not only the threat of nuclear catastrophes, whatever the cause, but the utter inability of humans to do anything about it for either the short or long term. For that reason, they are technological disasters brought on by human hubris and cupidity and the delusion that profit is good."

So why are they too dangerous? Is it the storage of radioactive materials?

"Yes and no, these plants self-destruct. Chernobyl is a good example. The reality is that the heat and the radiation levels generated by these plants not only destroys the coolant pipes and tubes visible and those buried in concrete, but also destroys the concrete surrounding them. Nuclear power is the singular most expensive means of generating power and the most threatening to the survival of man."

Then, why are more nuclear power plants being designed and politicians claiming they are badly needed to meet future demands?

"That's easy. The politicians benefit enormously from these so-called 'cost-effective' and extremely dangerous installations. They also live in the delusion that these NPP's are 'safe.' Nothing could be further from the truth. They will be dangerous for tens of thousands, possibly hundreds of thousands of years until they can stop the radiation from the decaying materials of uranium, plutonium, cesium, steel, copper, concrete, and stone."

I see why the Greek stories! We are doing Prometheus all over again, starting a fire that cannot be extinguished, which will ultimately destroy most living things around it. What I don't understand is why are the radioactive materials created by an NPP dangerous to animal and especially to human life?

"Radiation is caused by the decomposition of materials that give off energy as they die. When people talk of a half-life, they refer to the time it takes to decompose radioactivity of the material. The number of half-lives of radioactive materials may last only a few seconds or billions of years. It's the latter that are of concern because they can scramble the DNA of an animal and create hybrid or radical deformities, as found in certain cancers and birth defects.

Your scientists already know that because of the close relationship of calcium to strontium 90. Take a look at your Table of Elements.

"Human bodies cannot tell the difference between a deadly radioactive substance like Strontium 90 produced exclusively by NPP's and calcium found in milk or spinach. Radioactive iodine is known to lodge in the thyroid, upsetting the hormonal balance necessary to maintain good physical and mental health.

If Strontium 90 (created by nuclear power plants and bomb making industries) is indistinguishable to the human body from calcium, where to you think this deadly poison is going to go? Just look at the epidemic of cancers, brain cancer, the brain surrounded by a thick calcium-based skull, bone cancer and the rise in leukemia when the marrow of the bone is destroyed. Your medical professions call Leukemia a disease. It is more of a poisoning by radiation because human bodies interpret Strontium 90 as calcium; therefore, the rise in bone-marrow 'disease,' brain tumors, and breast cancers, any place the human body stores the calcium it receives, or Strontium 90, you bodies may mistakenly identify as calcium."

X, what you are telling me is really scary. I never heard of an explanation for a whole group of cancers before in terms of a mistake the human body makes by not distinguishing between calcium and a deadly radiation. So where does the strontium come from besides nuclear plants?

"Just think about it TED001. There were numerous above ground nuclear tests spreading radioactive isotopes all over the planet. It landed on grain fields, farm fields, on people, plants, and animals of every kind. Then there are nuclear disaster from Chernobyl to Fukushima. Once the event is over, humans think the problem has ended.

"Terrans absolutely must find solutions to the many issues related to radioactivity they have created in order to foster sustainable human life. The only way that objective will become possible will be if you begin to think and plan holographically, taking into account all of the possible consequences of every decision and action. Military planners have done this kind thought process for centuries. The great Chinese general Sun Tzu (Han Dynasty 206 BC - 220 AD) wrote about it, correctly observing his final conclusion about war strategies, if I may paraphrase: '*do not make war if you can avoid it.*'

"If you can succeed in the transition to holographic thinking and life-sustaining planning, you will become much more welcome into the galactic community and you will probably be alive and well enough to do so. It requires the utmost honesty, openness, transparency instead of profit-based and elitist-based secrecy. Your scientists and politicians are not priests and need to stop pretending to be the sanctioned and sole keepers of universal knowledge."

> You identify so many things we humans need to do just to rescue ourselves, I feel overwhelmed. It seems we need an *Encyclopedia Galactica* at this time in our history.
> On the other hand, I'm not sure I want to live in space ships or anything similar like your people apparently do, but I can't think of where to start to find a path to sustainability. Converting Mars into a habitable planet would be a major effort; we are in no way able to create space ships of the size and capabilities apparently constructed in yours. Those kinds of options would just be running away from the problems we have created for ourselves.

"We can help you. It will not be by any means familiar to you. We will not hold classes, hold your hands, or act as guides. As we are doing in this dialogue, we will intervene mostly by showing how your self-adopted and deluded yourselves into thinking what become sacrosanct thought processes. That means these assumptions are no-less self-destructive. Just by illustrating that there are three basic survival constructs humans have employed: a two-dimensional view of the world we call Planar; followed by a three-dimensional world identified as Vertical fixed on Place; there is a third, a four-dimensional Holographic society where Place is replaced by Interaction and Interconnection.

"All three of these dimensions of social structure are basic survival methods required by a host of conditions, from safe food production and health, to time-space technologies. Your mathematicians and physicists have speculated that there are dimensions in the universe that exist way beyond human understanding, even though your thoughts and exposure to external propaganda claim a spiritual world they know nothing about, except by adoption of authority based on an assumed and unverifiable authoritative pretext."

It seems like we should abandon all religions and cultural traditions, if what you say is the source of the problems we have.

"By no means abandon any traditions which constitute part of the communal Self, the health of a community and your individual selves. You are already holistic human beings trying to conform to artificial Vertical systems because you think there are no real alternatives.

"If you want to do something positive, first identify who in your current Vertical systems are there because they did not have the capacity for holistic thinking and are also identifiable sociopaths. These must include more than the occasional serial rapist or killers. Such sociopaths must never be in positions of leadership. Do not financially support institutions that have great undispersed wealth."

Like what?

"Anything that is cloaked in secrecy must be abandoned. Everything must be known by everyone at any time. This is what I meant by pan-dissemination of knowledge."

What if someone wanted to make a nuclear bomb?

"Everybody would know that so-and-so wants to make a destructive device appropriate entities would prevent it succeeding long before that person realized he could not make such a weapon himself."

Why do you focus on secrecy?

159

"Because, secrecy is the root of calumny and deceit. You cannot have a justice system that works in part in secret and the other part openly. That kind of duplicity does not wash."

> It would be hard to have a war if everyone knew everything everyone else is thinking. What about churches?

"You must bring to light any corporate wealth owned by religious institutions. In you Vertical ideology of 'freedom of religion' you hold the delusion that the intention of every religion and religious person means to do well for the rest of humanity. That is a very corrupting delusion to maintain as occurred in World War II when the Roman Catholic Church allied itself with Fascism and had its own army of foreign SS officers. Punish clerics who commit crimes against children, crimes against humanity, without exception. All religious property must be limited to the church, mosque, or synagogue, meeting place itself, applying strictly to the grounds on which that religious structure may stand. Owning daycare centers, old peoples' homes, hospitals, vast tracks of corporate farmland, cemeteries, bowling alleys, colleges and universities, and funeral homes have nothing to do with religion. They are just profit centers for an institution that has no responsibility to answer to your political managers.

"It is the function of the State of the World to protect all people throughout their lives and not because someone is doing charity work. Mean what you say when you declare something is or done for 'Life, liberty, and Freedom.'"

> Like the moneyless system? I cannot imagine how that can work. We get married in churches, have funerals in churches, places where the community can sanction or celebrate significant events in a common way. It seems churches do good things.

"Yes, using the naïve, the ignorant, and those who are obedient to the point they refuse to question anything, churches are places where things are done in a totally ineffective charitable way. There are innumerable examples where every transition in human life is done without religious sanctions.

If you can arrest your addiction for Magical Thinking, romantic sentimentality *ad nauseum*. Most importantly the formalistic Magico-Religious solutions to problems humans face must become consciously fought. If you can approach tragedies that occur absent reason or justice as something tragic, as simple as that, then just stop performing your magical prayers for miracles, and stop attending and supporting such institutional entities be they your local Disneyland, box-office, religion. Most importantly, do not give them any of your or anyone else's money or property. They cannot guarantee anyone will get to heaven when they can't prove there is one. It is the greatest human sham based on a Disneyland level of Magical Thinking will not sustain you momentary joy without a sober awareness of reality."

"What, for example, is magical about a wedding? People are making a commitment to each other for life. Yes, while the bride wears a white dress, symbolic since ancient Greek times of the sacrifice of her body to her husband as if she were a lamb on the altar or new slave, the property of the husband." However, your weddings are fantasies that have nothing to do with reality, least of all having responsibility to each other and your off-spring.

> Who doesn't know that the white gown the bride wears is not a testimony to her virginity even though that is what it is supposed to symbolize.

"Exactly, but what is not known is that bride's white clothing is the ancient symbol of sacrifice, in this custom the absolute sacrifice of the woman to her husband. In most Vertical Cultures females are owned like slaves by fathers and husbands. These are customs, TED. They constitute culture and are not the same worldwide. My invocation to you here is to rethink those products of Vertical Thinking and abandon self-destructive notions. They may not seem like delusions until you investigate and realize where these institutions and ideologies spring from the Vertical Christmas tree, as it were. In each case, you will be shaking off oppression that is costing millions of you human unlimited stress and suffering. In one form or another, you will be abandoning your many Vertical layers of slavery endowed by delusional, self-destructive concepts. That is real freedom."

By deduction I can tell a little bit about your lives and culture, but I would like to know more about how it works.

"We are sensible enough to know that we cannot give you the '*Encyclopedia Galactica*,' as your people call it. Perhaps just these small changes to break down the Vertical layers of psychological, social, and physical slavery will somehow help."

LOG XVII

CONFESSIONS OF X:
PEERING THROUGH ALIEN PRISMS

I keep trying to conceive how old your civilization is, your social structure, how decisions are made, what are your responses if a nuclear war began here, or an attack was made on an EVC again as at Roswell and as I understand is even frequently done now by secret installations of weaponry. How do you feel about the recent attack from an American air base in central Australia, where a laser beam was shot at an EVC flying with others at a great distance from earth?

"TED I have attempted to make it apparent to you that Terrans have much to clean up on their own planet, most of it about your thought processes. The technical solutions are easy, so it is no surprise that you value these most at the present time as a measure of everything. Unfortunately, your focus is so intellectually blinding that the most difficult tasks are disposing yourselves of Magical Thinking, Vertical Social systems, and the false sanctification claimed and attributed to in objects, people, places, and ideologies.

"You have entered the Molecular or Holographic Age as if you were walking into a room backward and there is no turning back. Turn around your thinking. You can make the transitions less painful or less violent, or, in you desperation to hold onto the fantasies and delusions of Vertical tradition, you may dissolve your planet into the fire you most religiously fear.

"I want to assure you about some things, most of which you may find surprising about our civilization and your emergence into it. I will list them in a random order, so that you realize one is no more valuable than another.

"If you solve the major thought problems you now face, I can promise your life will not become boring. You will find so many challenges, new, 'mind-blowing,' wonderful things about your and others' lives and living experiences, that you will wonder why you could have held onto so many primitive and self-destructive notions that kept you in a prison of the mind for so long. So, here's a list of promises.

"You will find ways to cure all the diseases, biological, viral, known to man and how to eat and do things that keep you at optimal health.

"If you begin to realize the second claim I am making, you will live longer and more fruitful lives, each human being finding the special gifts the universe has genetically and in the fruit of time bestowed upon each of you individually and in terms of your families of origin.

"Warfare will cease to exist and the need to create wars for profit or for any other reason, especially revenge.

"You will dispose of a money-based, for-profit society, replacing it with the intrinsic value of human life and the natural global environment you have inherited and adopt a less earth-destroying system.

"You will eventually be welcomed into the galactic community and into the secrets and known history of the universe about which your scientists and millions of others would like to know much more about and experience.

"All people on earth will have access to limitless free energy to meet their needs.

"All people on earth will live in abundance, with forms of nourishment coming to everyone from many healthful sources and to which everyone will be given access.

"Your preoccupation with death and the elaborate funerary costs for preparation for death, funerals, images of commemoration, all will become unnecessary. Any who so chooses may be buried at sea, on the planet, or returned to their origins in the sun.

"You will solve the vast majority of genetic, sociological, and traumatic reasons for mental illness and mental dysfunctionality.

"Governance and law will be self-evident as all human beings will have the same information, genetic disposition and will honor laws in the clear awareness that they have been tested on millions of iterations to validate their purpose.

"Information, every idea and thought is available to everyone everywhere. There are no publishing hierarchies nor informational hierarchies, or keepers of state secrets.

"Spy agencies will become obsolete.

"Secrecy, secret courts, secret prisons, secret laws, and secret punishments will become obsolete and as they are rejected for the inhumanity that they bring to humankind.

"Machines of war will be converted to productive materials, a very old promise, but one you can still keep."

That's it? Which comes first? Where do we start? Are we going to have help from Galactic Entities?

"You always have. We may also take measures to raise intelligence levels. You have a tendency to produce millions of low I.Q. slave and slave-substitute individuals you mistakenly thought you needed for heavy labor, thus lowering the capacity of the human race to survive. While you claim human life is sacred, you attempt to balance out the disproportionate numbers of numbskulls by exterminating them in your inevitable religious, racial, and territorial wars."

How will we do that, by telepathy?

"Unlikely, more like genetic/DNA interventions. As for what you label telepathy, you already know that you know some things as they are happening even though you are not in the same place as the event taking place. It is part of your mind that will be developed over centuries, until, like my species, it will be your primary form of communication."

These changes or interventions are done by abduction?

"In some isolated cases. Abductions are really unnecessary to perpetuate positive changes in the human species. We will have to address that issue at another time, as your limited 'histories' of abductions by EBE's paint a very dark picture, one that we must warn you about."

Abductions seems to be really wrong, unethical, a kind of rape.

"You put a patient to sleep for an operation, correct? They recall nothing of the medical staff taking over their life functions. Do you remember your abduction TED001?"

Didn't know I had one!

"Do you feel raped, molested?"

I'm not a lawyer, but it doesn't seem right. If I was. When did that happen?

"We changed your DNA so you would live a little longer. Now how do you feel about that?"

Is that true? I guess I would feel better if you had made me a little more intelligent.

"We did that too, a little."

People pray to God for these kinds of things. Do you ever answer prayers? Wait, why only 'a little?'

"Rarely, and no explanations or comments are going to be made other than what has already been said."

But you might make changes to people who do not know they are being 'upgraded,' so to speak. Maybe they are not. Maybe they are abducted just to be eaten.

"Making changes without abductions, yes, sometimes millions. As I said, let's save the negative and fear-based events for later. We will eventually get to it."

Is it always an upgrade we receive? Because most of us ARE going to feel raped if it is not.

"No comment. You ask too many questions, redundant ones at that, and your fear lies too close to the surface. Do you feel 'raped' when a Dentist pulls a tooth and replaces it with an artificial one?"

Yes, perhaps my fear does get intense, but I would like to see for myself all the achievements you claim your peoples have made. I would like to think these are all realistic, achievable goals. I would like to meet you too X.

"We have already met even though I am over two-billion miles away from earth at the present, somewhere near the planet you call Neptune."

You mean we have met through this dialogue?

"No, we have met in person, but I can never reveal myself to you or to any other alien in such encounters. We are different, but look in the mirror in your bathroom and you will see we are similar in all physical features. We have a common ancestry, a common DNA, we are both sexually identifiable as male and female, we love the experience of beauty in all of its forms. Those among our race are tall, have ideal physiognomic bodies, ideal proportions like yourselves, have slightly larger brains, but it's something you will grow into liking and having, we hope.

"It has been my pleasure, TED001.Out"

I hope you're not signing off...are you? X, X, come back. I have more questions. What about the first solar society, the multi-million year-old glass domes on the moon? I want you to tell me more about good aliens and, and if there are horrific and bad ones. Damn. X. Why did you leave?

At that point I kept hitting the Return key, tapping almost hysterically, hoping he or she would answer. In the days, weeks, and months since we last communicated, I have heard nothing, nor have I felt like writing. I have even felt like crying on my keyboard at times, but the thought of shorting it out reminded me of what happened once when I spilled some coke on it.

Then my dog started whimpering. I had to take her out again for her nightly bladder relief but unlike her, I look at the stars and wonder where X came from, who the other visitors are, what they are like, if they all have good intentions or even care. Most disappointing, since our last communication, I have noticed that not a lot has changed in the human community on this spaceship called earth. Not much at all. The most despicable warfare, violence on people on people on every branch of human existence, the destruction of the world by Global Warming by for-profit profiteers. Suicidal rationalizations that defy all scientific evidence.

167

My dog hasn't changed much either. When I take her for a pee in the night, she howls at the moon after relieving herself, as her wolf ancestors still do. When I stare up at the stars as my ancient ancestors did and wonder where in the heavens X and his PoO are located, I feel very much alone probably as my ancestors once did when they heard the voices of God, of their many gods, their angels, those beings that fill up the vast emptiness of space and time. I wonder about those who know the emptiness of our hearts, our hunger 'to know,' our desire to know truth, to know more about us and those in the vast reaches of space, time, an awareness of who we are a part and still not yet a part.

X has convinced me that that full entry into the galaxy and universe will not come until we move or evolve out of our Vertical, gravity-bound, ups and downs, highers and lowers, and put our Places in a new kind of space, where those worthless things and ideas we hold so absolutely dear will either be discarded for the nonsense they are or retained as those intrinsically shared in the unity of all things.

ADDENDA

LATENT RECONNECTIONS

A Strange Encounter

It was about two A.M. in that part of the desert. It is a four-lane highway, known as Interstate 8, near the dunes before you get to Yuma. There is nothing but sand, sage brush, and creosote in this part of the southern California desert.

For some reason I felt wide awake, thinking of what I would do with my children during their vacation with me in San Diego. I saw a large helicopter flying toward me on the other side of the freeway, but couldn't see its shape very well. There was no moonlight and the aircraft was also dark. I figured it was a Highway Patrol helicopter and I slowed down to the speed limit.

As it approached, I slowed down more to get a better look. It also slowed down a little too, giving me a chance to see that it was walnut shaped, had no landing wheels and no propellers, none of which bothered me until I realized the only noise I could hear was that of my car rushing through the wind.

My heart began beating harder. I was thinking I might be having a close encounter, looked at my watch, and sped up as the craft continued on toward the West while I bolted down the freeway eastward as fast as my car would go in the opposite direction from the walnut. Remembering Barney & Betty Hill and their abduction for several hours they could not account for, I looked at my watch. Only a minute or two had passed since encountering the craft and we came parallel to each other, so I knew I had not been abducted as the Hills had been and felt relieved.

Not only that, this flying walnut did not look like a flying saucer, nor anything like the large cigar shape my grandparents once saw hovering over the Victorville Air Force Base one evening when they were heading west on Highway 66 to Victorville. By the shape alone, I dismissed my own anxiety over this strange encounter with the floating black walnut and drove on to Tucson to pick up my kids for summer vacation. Desert tales are always mysterious until the accumulation of disparate information links them together.

The Military-Industrial Complex Answers to a Government Investor

My grandfather, Elmer Cook, also worked at Edwards (Muroc) AFB as a water cooler repairman, where in the 1940's the latest aircraft designed by Lockheed's 'Skunk Works' and Northrop were test flown. He was one of the hundreds of people and military personnel working at Edwards required by Secretary of War, Stimson, to witness the fleet of 'flying wings' blown up. It turns out when the contract was awarded, Stimson had invested in a company that was supposed to get the contract but didn't. Furthermore, Stimson did not like Mr. Northrop who could be a crusty entrepreneur. My grandfather and others were required to watch this exhibit of destruction, never understanding why the most advanced aircraft produced by American technology were so strangely being blown to pieces. Public announcements simply said the flying wing was abandoned because they were *'unstable causing one to crash.'*

On the Other Side of the Mojave River (ca. 1954?) "A Giant Flying Cigar"

At one of our Thanksgiving dinners, just like many others, was a time when around the table jokes were heard and stories told. One of those told by my Step-Grandfather Cook and defended by my Grandmother, was this:

As my grandparents were driving one evening from their home near Hodge just off of Highway 66 toward George Air Force Base where my grandfather worked in the 1950's, they saw an extremely large cigar-shaped thing that seemed to be hovering above the base. They were frightened by its huge size but knew by its shape it was nothing coming out of the 'Skunk Works' or Northrop. When my grandparents told us about what they had seen that late afternoon, my parents were incredulous. At 13 or 14 I didn't think such a thing was possible, but at the same time believed my grandparents were always truthful and that they must have seen something few other human beings had ever witnessed. I never forgot their Thanksgiving Dinner story.

Thinking of that encounter, I was standing one time among one of the scattered creosote bush-covered knolls behind my grandparents' house. With the wind whistling through the brush, I had my own remote 'encounter.' To the South of their house was a large expanse of desert with two mountains in the distance with a V-shaped space between them. Then, in that space between the two mountains, a silver object was flying East to West but at an incredibly slow pace. I knew it wasn't a jet. It seemed like it was globular, which I attributed to the distance. I watched for it to cross the V-shaped space between the two mountains, disappearing behind the larger one. I waited for it to come out on the west side of the larger mountain, but it never did. I recalled this remote encounter recently after starting the second edition of this book.

In the 1950's there was much anxiety about aliens, based on conflicting information about the Barney and Betty Hill abduction and the Roswell events. Only in 2012 when I learned (a) that large cigar-shaped Extraterrestrial Vehicular Craft's were commonplace as EVC sightings and (b) that a special meeting was set up with aliens in 1954 to meet with President Eisenhower at Muroc (Edwards) Air Force Base to work out an agreement, did I make the connection with my grandparents story.

Once I connected the two encounters, which occurred at about the same time. My grandparents did perhaps see a large cigar-shaped EVC. It does not mean that this was the same craft that delivered the GE's to the conference with President Dwight Eisenhower. It might have been the main ship used to bring the craft that did fly to Edwards. Because the aircraft my Grandparents saw had no wings or propulsion exhaust, they thought it must be another experimental craft or another worldly alien one.

Given the overwhelming volume of evidence and credible testimony left by dying and retiring military, a full disclosure about EVC's and any Alien/ U.S. agreement must be made available to all people on the planet, if such an encounter "of the third kind" did occur. As for the hypotheses about potential psychological effects on society and religion I think they must be dismissed as unworthy of speculation and secrecy. If religions fail in the face of external realities, then it merely demonstrates the fragility of Vertical based religions and the world will be a better place in the absence of social acceptance of institutionalized Magical Thinking.

Understandably, such official admissions may have far-reaching psychological, philosophical, especially religious reactions. he human race needs to know and understand the reasons for this manifestation on a scale never before witnessed. We have a right to know. Without it, we are at the mercy of those who would misuse this information for their personal and sectarian group advantage over the general human population of earth. Withholding information and secrecy based on assumptions of Magical Thinking processes is tantamount to a crime. If these keepers lie as the primary source of disappearances, deaths of those who knew the truth, or the murder of our President Kennedy and other members of his family, they must be brought before U.S. and the International court in The Hague for crimes against humanity.

To delude ourselves or to be deluded by others must be at the forefront of every person who values their life and their families whose futures and those of everyone on this spaceship are at stake.

A circular coded message left in one of the "crop circles" in England said only: *Beware of those bearing gifts. We must leave.* According to Colonel Corso who revealed in *The Day After Roswell* how technology reverse-engineered from alien craft and captured aliens, was sent to him by military intelligence. It was his task to disseminate among public universities and private institutions new technologies that have since become the foundation of the 'Computer Age' in all of its ramifications.

What this has to mean is that those things that have initially given advantages to American industry and technology have an equally dark side. That dark side is the information we are not given, surely the most important information that I and millions of others believe we have the right to know. What was that agreement, if any, made with aliens to capture (abduct) innocent people? Is there a global agreement among nations? Is the U.S. military shooting down alien ships? Have aliens double-crossed the so-called agreements made with Presidents Eisenhower and earlier with Truman? Are there good and bad Aliens and, if so, which are which? Have we received "gifts" from encounters with a race of EBE's of the worst kind?

Since the 1947 destruction of one or two alien craft, details of that information is unknown. Were those alien craft carrying only children as one author suggests? Did they come to keep us from preventing nuclear war since they showed up at the place where we set off the first "atomic bomb" at "Trinity" site, White Sands, New Mexico and putatively shut down U.S. and Russian nuclear missile systems? What is information and mis-information in this conflicting mass of theories and leaks of data, based on 'authorities' where we have little or no verifiability? Has a cabal of the "military-intelligence-industrial-complex" cited by Eisenhower taken over the United States government? Is it the "secret government" George Bush junior in another manifestation of unwitting commentary revealed the "New World Order?" He also spoke of it after the 'twin towers' and 'Building 5' were mined and destroyed killing nearly 3,000 lives? Was it a strategy of a cabal governed by fear and ignorance that plunged Americans into another unnecessary war "for peace and freedom", or another grab at energy sources in the form of gas and oil? If the former Canadian minister of defense openly admits the encounters with aliens, why should we believe any 'official nay-sayers.'

Until all of these questions can be answered with absolutely verifiable evidence and certainty can any one believe in anything professed before us and to our children from the earliest grades to the latest? Those who are keeping these secrets and using them for their own purposes of 'power-over' in bald-faced deceit and duplicity must be brought to justice, critical to not only the people of the United States but to the entire population of earth. Or is the larger question really about who is manipulating who? Are we being manipulated by a hostile alien species who have born us those "gifts" we have been forewarned to "beware"?

If so, is there, are there good alien races or an alliance of "good" visitors who bear us no harm, or a singularly dangerous one? I have preferred in this book to see what it might look like if we were being mentored by a superior race belonging to the galactic community, of which we are only one. I have chosen to think my 'mentor X' wants for us to simply 'grow up,' to dispose of our incredulous delusions; for us to look beyond technologies of force and destruction to become part of the vast galactic community and for our evolved progeny to inherit Ezekiel's *"everlasting highlands"* for unknown millennia to come.

To dispose ourselves of Magical Thinking, to avoid and cease to support the sources of such delusions by political and religious fantasizers are the first steps. To truly lateralize (democratize) all Vertical institutions as much as we can, we will create true democracies and diminish the authority our absolutists of Vertical thinkers. We need no religious or imperialist 'pontiff' to act as the 'bridge' between 'heaven and earth,' and realize our collective imperative to unseat such dangerous Verticalists, forever pledging to never allow any human, animal, or environment, to be subjected to such hierarchical buffoonery or abuse of the human body, mind, and spirit, or abuse and destruction of our life-giving and sustaining planet.

www.ingramcontent.com/pod-product-compliance
Lightning Source LLC
Chambersburg PA
CBHW070903290526
45795CB00001B/219